**Donated
To The Library by**

LLOYD FALLERS

c/o Barry & Winnifred
Sullivan

August, 2004

ROBINS SERIES
No 2

TRADE AND TRAVEL IN EARLY BAROTSELAND

Robins Series

No. 1 Zambezia and Matabeleland in the Seventies

No. 42

No. 84

No. 78

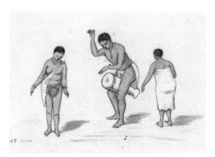

No. 64

For captions please see page v

TRADE AND TRAVEL
IN EARLY
BAROTSELAND

The Diaries of George Westbeech
1885–1888
AND
Captain Norman MacLeod
1875–1876

ILLUSTRATED WITH
THE SKETCHES OF
Lieutenant William Fairlie

EDITED BY
Edward C. Tabler
M.S.

1963
UNIVERSITY OF CALIFORNIA PRESS
BERKELEY AND LOS ANGELES

Published in
the United States of America
by the University of California Press
of Berkeley and Los Angeles, California
Published in Great Britain by
Chatto & Windus Ltd.
42 William IV Street
London W.C.2.

Printed in Great Britain

No. 42

Run to a Stand Still. 31st May

Mounted hunters coursed giraffes until they tired, then galloped up alongside and killed by firing into the shoulder ; or they dismounted and drove a heavy bullet through the animals' body by firing into its stern. This giraffe seems to be accepting its fate resignedly, though sometimes one might be aggressive and try to defend itself by striking out with its forelegs.

No. 84

Pookoo

The puka (*Onotragus leche*), a water antelope smaller than the lechwe and less aquatic in its habits. It ranges from Ngamiland through Northern Rhodesia. It was discovered by Oswell and Livingstone on the Botletle River in 1849.

No. 78

The Elephant Hunt. Zambesi

A scene from the annual elephant hunt conducted by the Barotse to obtain ivory for their King. This one, which was attended by MacLeod, Fairlie, Cowley, and Dorehill, was held in the angle between the Chobe and Zambezi rivers. The base of the triangle was closed by fire, hunters were stationed in canoes at the river banks to turn the quarry from the water, and beaters drove the herds towards waiting hunters. Several hundred men took part in this hunt, which was held from about 27 to 30 October 1875. Several hunters were usually killed by the elephants when they broke through the cordons, or by the wild shooting of their fellows.

No. 64

Girls Dancing. At Sejoro

Barotse girls dance intermittently for days as part of their puberty rites, but these females seem to be merely amusing themselves.

CONTENTS

LIST OF ILLUSTRATIONS

LIST OF ILLUSTRATIONS

MAPS

PREFACE

THE present rapid spread of nationalistic ideals among the indigenous peoples of tropical Africa is lending political cohesion to populations which appeared up to a decade or so ago to be fragmented irreconcilably by tribal loyalties. It is giving them also a better appreciation of their own values, greater independence to conduct their own affairs, and is focussing a new interest on the necessity for a better understanding of Africa's peoples and their problems.

The accompanying revival and reorientation of interest in African history is hardly to be wondered at, therefore, and is resulting in a re-examination of the published source material, renewed search for unpublished manuscripts, and a new consideration of the traditional oral records. These sources, together with that derived from archaeological excavations, are now being used, not as heretofore, to trace the history of the expansion of European colonial enterprise in Africa, but to write the history of the peoples who inhabit that continent.

This second volume in the Robins Series contains records not previously published of considerable interest for the history of the Barotse peoples and of the Barotse Protectorate.

The diary of George Westbeech, who is described by his editor as 'the man responsible for establishing a British foothold in Barotseland,' deserved much earlier publication. That it has not appeared in print before is partly due to the unsuccessful attempt to trace an earlier diary which it is believed he must have kept. If such still exists today, it is to be hoped that the present volume will bring it to light, for this, together with the full diary of MacLeod, which also is missing, would amplify considerably our knowledge of details of happenings and personalities in the Barotse Valley in the '70s.

Livingstone, in the 1850s, was the first to describe Barotseland and its people, then under the dominance of the Makalolo. Westbeech takes up the story again some twenty years later and through his diary carries Barotse history down to the establishment of the Paris Mission stations by the Rev. François Coillard and records many details of the confused events after the death of his friend

xi

King Sipopa and the succession of Lewanika to the Chieftainship. Westbeech spent the last seventeen years of his life among the Barotse. As seen through his diary and the writings of his contemporaries, he stands out as a man of great personal integrity. While strict as to discipline and expecting obedience, he was always essentially a kindly man. The personal glimpses that we have of him helping his less fortunate fellows – with wagons, oxen, food, or intercessions with the King – or nursing a dying man when his own health was in little better state, endear him to us as a man kindly disposed to all who sought his help, one who enjoyed his life to the full, who was ever a good friend to the Barotse, and for whom the Barotse had the greatest respect.

Westbeech and MacLeod give us many insights into the everyday life of the Barotse and of the day to day experiences of the traveller and hunter in south-central Africa during the 1870s, but these verbal descriptions are even more vividly set before us in the sketches of MacLeod's brother officer Fairlie, who has indeed left us a unique record of King Sipopa and his times.

We are most fortunate to have again E. C. Tabler, the well-known authority on nineteenth century travel in south-central Africa, to edit this volume. His Introduction and knowledge of the events and lives of the European traders, hunters, miners, and missionaries mentioned in the diaries has set these latter in their right perspective and has added greatly to the interest of the texts themselves.

As I have now taken up an appointment at the University of California, this will be the last volume in the Robins Series for which I shall act as general-editor. It is with much regret that I relinquish these duties, and I wish Gervas Clay, my successor at the Rhodes-Livingstone Museum and in the editorship, every success. If he derives as much pleasure from his association with the editors of future volumes and in seeing the texts through the press as I have had from the first two, then his task will indeed be an enjoyable and a rewarding one.   *J. Desmond Clark*
Department of Anthropology
September, 1961   University of California

INTRODUCTION

I

T H E Barotse, or Lozi, are a Bantu tribe living on the upper Zambezi River in North Western Rhodesia. Originally from northern Angola, they migrated to their present home via the headwaters of the Kabompo River, a tributary of the upper Zambezi, perhaps in the eighteenth century. The name *Barotse* was given them by their conquerors, the Makololo; they once called themselves A-Luyi, Men of the River, and their old language, Siluyana, which was superseded by Sikololo, continued to be used as a court language by the royal family and the headmen. Their home is the Barotse Valley, which is really a level plain fifty to sixty miles wide, beginning a short distance above the Gonye Falls and extending more than one hundred miles to the north of Lealui. The overflow of the Zambezi in summer inundates the flood plain, and it is capable of supporting a relatively large population because of its fertility.

The Barotse developed a government and political organization much superior to that of most of the Southern Bantu. They had an unwritten and rudimentary constitution and a tightly knit administrative system. Their King was a tyrant and absolute monarch who often ruled in oppressive fashion, though he was frequently deposed when his cruelties became excessive. He was assisted by a council of advisers, the principal of whom was a sort of prime minister called the Ngambela. The country was divided into districts, each one ruled by a Lozi appointed by the King, and even the village headmen were chosen by him. The Barotse were farmers and pastoralists with a riverine economy, and they were expert smiths and woodworkers. Their superior physique, intellect, and cohesiveness enabled them to extend their sovereignty over a large number of other tribes who greatly outnumbered them.

By the 1840's the Barotse had stretched their hegemony (at least that of the raid) eastwards of the Victoria Falls, and they ruled in the south to the Zambezi and Chobe rivers. Some Mambunda came into Barotseland under two chiefs and voluntarily accepted Barotse rule and were therefore exempt from paying tribute. They were the official magicians and excelled in the making of mats and baskets. The Masubia, boatmen, fishermen, and potters, lived on the Chobe River and on both sides of the Zambezi from the Chobe mouth up to Katonga Village. The Matotela, boatbuilders and smiths, were centrally located between the Zambezi and the Kafue. The Mankoya of the Luena and Luampa valleys in Mankoya District lived by hunting and gathering and used bows and poisoned arrows. These were the principal subject tribes, and the nearer sections of the Mashukulumbwe (BaꞮla) of the Kafue Valley and the Mampukushu and Mashi on the Kwando paid tribute to the Barotse.

II

The conquests of Tshaka, founder of the Zulu power, caused great disruptions of the Bantu in southeastern Africa during the early nineteenth century. Hordes of people of Sotho stock, homeless, starving, and disorganized, fugitives from raids and wars, invaded southern Bechuanaland during the 1820's. An advanced group was defeated and turned back in June 1823 at Dithakong by the Griquas, who thus saved the northern stations of the London Missionary Society and prevented an invasion of the Cape Colony. Another group, originally a few hundred people of the Fokeng, hived off and, under a leader of great natural ability, one Sebetwane, began a long journey to the north in search of a home. Sebetwane was not a chief by birth, but he made himself one by his bravery and capacity for ruling, talents that were soon matured by the necessity for survival. His people, gaining strength by adding captives to their ranks and by the voluntary adherence of the dispossessed, made their slow way northwards through Bechuanaland. The details of this anabasis are lost, but it is said that Sebetwane defeated all the Bechuana tribes and settled for a time among the Kwena, near present-day Molepolole. The Matabele, recent deserters from Tshaka under Mzilikazi, invaded the western

Transvaal and defeated Sebetwane, who with his followers retreated to Lake Ngami. There they conquered the Tawana, but,
not liking the lake district, they soon moved north across the
Chobe.

Sebetwane subdued the Masubia and Batoka and settled first
on the healthful uplands north and east of the Zambezi. He was
not permitted to rest there long, however, for his old enemies the
Matabele, driven by the Voortrekkers from the Transvaal to the
high plateau between the Zambezi and the Limpopo, found him
and sent warriors who attacked him. In order to protect himself,
Sebetwane made for the upper Zambezi. The Barotse king Mulambwa (Marambwa) had died not long before and rival claimants
ruling in the north and south caused an outbreak of civil war over
the succession. This state of things, common enough in the tribe,
made it easy for Sebetwane and his Makololo to conquer the
Barotse-Mambunda people and become their rulers. Other Matabele raids followed, so that Sebetwane moved to Linyanti in the
marshes of the Chobe River. He was safe there behind the rivers,
for the Matabele were not watermen, and he was living among the
Masubia and the Batoka and could prevent them from helping
the enemy.

III

It was at Linyanti that the Makololo first made contact with the
British. William Cotton Oswell and David Livingstone reached
the Chobe in 1851 and penetrated as far as Old Sesheke on the
Zambezi. Livingstone was much taken with Sebetwane, whom the
missionary characterizes as strong and wise, and indeed Livingstone saw virtues in the Makololo that other travellers were unable
to find. Sebetwane died of pneumonia while his visitors were with
him, and a son named Sekeletu succeeded. Sekeletu was a great
favourite of Livingstone's, and that chief's help enabled the explorer to make his first great journey across the continent. But
under Sekeletu, who was weak and foolish, the Makololo degene-
rated, and when he died in 1864 a relative named Mbololo became
chief in his place.

The new ruler was so extremely cruel that, when a rival claimant appeared, the latter found much support and civil war broke out. The tribe was further weakened by losses in these fights and by defections to the Matabele and the Tawana, and the Barotse saw their chance and took it. Sipopa (the Sepopa of the Diaries) a son of Mulambwa, who was already in the north in what is now the Kabompo district, sent his army under his Ngambela Njekwa against the Makololo and conquered them with ease. Most of the Makololo males were killed, others escaped to neighbouring tribes, and some were spared; the women and children were incorporated into the Lozi and other tribes. It was the end of the Makololo as a nation, but their mark remained. The Barotse adopted their language and married their women. Sipopa was chosen as their ruler by the victorious Barotse. He immediately reasserted his sovereignty over the Batoka and made his position more secure by having two of his three brothers killed.

IV

British traders very soon followed Oswell and Livingstone to the Chobe River and attempted to do business with the Makololo. A Portuguese trader from Angola, Silva Porto, had visited the Barotse before their subjection by the Makololo, and the tribes of the upper Zambezi bought their European goods from the Mambari, half-caste traders from Bihé in Angola. Because those merchants bought slaves, Livingstone wanted the tribes to trade with the British from the south, who, however, were not encouraged to come in by the Makololo and the Barotse. The Mambari sold cheaper goods and had a shorter distance over which to transport them, and the British were badly treated and usually not permitted to go beyond the line of the Chobe and Zambezi rivers; it may have been that the riverine peoples feared that the Matabele would learn from the southern traders how to get at them. The London Missionary Society tried to realize Livingstone's other desire, that of having teachers in the country, but the mission party that reached Linyanti in 1860 were nearly all killed by fever and the survivors retreated. Except for Livingstone, who after his departure for the east coast in 1855 visited the Makololo only once more, in 1860, British influence north of the Zambezi and the Chobe was nonexistent. Attempts to trade beyond those rivers were made during the 1860's, but without success.

V

The man responsible for establishing a British foothold in Barotseland was an Englishman named George Westbeech, who was not a political agent or an evangelist but a trader, an occupation that was often much maligned in Southern Africa. Facts about his life and origins are difficult to find, though his doings in the interior are chronicled by several hunters, explorers, and missionaries. He emigrated to Natal in 1862 and a year or two later made a trading journey to Matabeleland, at about the same time that George Arthur ('Elephant') Phillips first visited that country. The two men formed a partnership that was to last as long as Westbeech lived, and while the latter operated the business in Zambezia, Phillips lived in Matabeleland and managed that branch of the enterprise till he retired to London in 1890. They traded with the Matabele during the 1860's, and they gained the confidence of the old king Mzilikazi and of the future king, Lobengula, through their integrity and manliness. In 1868 the partners made a remarkable journey; they accompanied Lobengula and a Matabele regiment over the Hunyani River in Mashonaland and past Wata's Kraal to the headwaters of the Mazoe, and down that stream to its tributary the Inyagu. They entered the Matabele country in January 1870 and attended Lobengula's coronation, and in March Westbeech and another man trekked south to Hopetown to obtain trade goods. He was at Tati again in August 1870, when he went south with four wagons, apparently to prepare for his first venture to the Zambezi.

Westbeech and George Blockley arrived at the Chobe-Zambezi junction in 1871 with three wagons loaded with goods. Sipopa came with a large retinue to visit the strangers, and he soon told the white men to remove their personal belongings from the vehicles; he then had the goods offloaded and taken to a town over the river. Westbeech soon followed his goods and made friends with the King, who detained him a year and a half in order to enjoy his company and cement the friendship. When the trader left, Sipopa filled his wagons with ivory and wept at his going. Westbeech profited in the amount of about £12,000 on this journey, which determined him to continue as a trader to the Barotse. He returned to the country in 1872, when he brought up another helper, Dr. Benjamin Frederick Bradshaw, a former ship's doctor interested in natural history, who for six years managed Westbeech's station at Pandamatenga and became well known, with Blockley, as a knowledgeable Zambezi hand who extended hospitality and help to all travellers.

Westbeech spent seventeen years, the rest of his life, among the Barotse, with infrequent journeys to the healthful south to renew his stocks of supplies and trade goods. During 1873 he travelled to the Zambezi and the Barotse Valley and remained as Sipopa's guest till June 1874, and he did not go south again till the beginning of the next year. At the end of August 1875 he arrived at Pandamatenga from Shoshong with his bride, the daughter of a Transvaal farmer whom he had married a few months before, and a large party. They visited Sipopa at Sesheke and saw the Victoria Falls, and Westbeech journeyed south again during February and March 1876. He was at Jacobsdal in the Orange Free State about October 1876, en route to the Zambezi, where he lived throughout 1877, when his wife visited him there. Westbeech may have been in England in late 1878 and 1879, for we next hear of him in Barotseland during the winter of 1882, when he helped the Scots missionary Arnot into the country. He was there during nearly the whole of the succeeding two years. The diary he kept tells his story from his return to his adopted land in 1885 almost to the end of his life.

Westbeech was well educated and had excellent manners and many cultured qualities. He was generous and helpful to all Europeans who came to see the Falls and explore and hunt, and all of them who entered Barotseland and were extended privileges there owed such special rights to Westbeech or his agents. He was

6

popular with everyone, black and white alike, for his bravery and friendliness. He must have been made of iron to have survived so many summers in the malarial Zambezi Valley, constantly on the move, living on coarse and bad food, and exposed to the weather. By 1878 he had had fever more than thirty times, and he used to say jokingly that he never felt well without at least a touch of it.

The trader's hold over Sipopa and Lewanika can be explained. Revolt and assassination were ever present in Barotse politics, and the King could trust no one of his own people to any great extent. It was therefore a great thing for him to have a friend who could be trusted completely, someone who could be depended upon to give disinterested advice and to keep his word. The white and half-caste Angolans could not meet these requirements, nor could they be relied on not to take part in conspiracies. There was no doubt about Westbeech's integrity, and he was even able to have his notes accepted by Africans in payment for goods and services ; he and his agents faithfully redeemed them and thus established for themselves a credit system. Westbeech was one of the few white men really intimate with Lobengula, and through his great influence with the Matabele king was able to prevent Matabele raids on the Barotse, which added greatly to his stature. That he was fluent in the Sesuto, Sindebele, and Sechuana languages must have been of considerable help to Westbeech in his dealings with the tribes.

Westbeech and Blockley were the first Europeans after Livingstone to ascend very far the upper Zambezi, and until Sipopa's death they were the only whites permitted to enter Barotseland and travel freely there. Sipopa gave his friend standing permission to hunt elephants anywhere in the country, and the Englishman sent from ten to fifteen tons of ivory downcountry every year till that ruler's death. Westbeech was recognized by both the Matabele and the Barotse as headman of Pandamatenga, he became a member of the Barotse council of state, and he was looked up to by all the tribesmen he knew as the equal of their chiefs. His operations extended to the wild Mashukulumbwe people and to the Mashi groups on the Kwando. Among other things they did that helped open the country, the trader and his men continually improved and shortened the wagon roads to the Zambezi from Tati and Shoshong, and he established a postal service of African runners from Shoshong to Pandamatenga. Westbeech had at first to compete with many half-caste Portuguese traders, all slave and ivory buyers, and he beat them out and established a near-monopoly by bringing in better goods and by ingratiating himself with chiefs and headmen. His activities tended to reduce the slave trade by substituting other commerce for it, and he did much to raise the British name in the eyes of the Africans. The upshot of all this was that Portuguese influence with the Barotse was neutralized and British influence firmly established.

VI

Sipopa, like all the Barotse kings of the nineteenth century, was a despot given to summary punishment for the slightest offense—one of his favourite pastimes was feeding the crocodiles at Sesheke with human beef. He became increasingly cruel and arbitrarily set aside customary law, and as a result there was a rebellion late in 1876. The King escaped the rebels but was shot by a trusted follower; he made his way downriver by canoe to the Chobe mouth and then overland to the Victoria Falls, in an attempt to reach safety with Westbeech at Pandamatenga. But he became too ill to travel and sent for the trader, a message to which Westbeech was able to respond only in time to see his black friend die.

Mamili the Ngambela who had raised the rebellion against Sipopa put Mwanawina, a grandson of Mulambwa, on the throne. Within a year there was a further rebellion and Mwanawina was driven out and replaced by Lubosi, another grandson of Mulambwa, in 1878. In 1884 Lubosi was driven into exile and his cousin Akafuna Tatila was chosen in his place. However, after a short interregnum Lubosi fought his way back to power and took the name of Lewanika, becoming the greatest king of the Barotse. Shrewd and capable, he restored order and regained ascendency over the subject tribes and extended his rule until he governed an area in Central Africa larger than France. Although he never embraced Christianity, he became moderate in his rule under the good influence of Coillard and the other French Protestant missionaries. Coillard took Westbeech's place in Lewanika's regard after the death of the trader, and the missionary was largely responsible for the King's placing his country under British protection in 1890.

Westbeech's diary is a valuable record of a critical period in Barotse history, a time when it was uncertain which claimant would become king and during which Lewanika was struggling to consolidate his position. Westbeech supported Lewanika, though he was careful to keep on as good terms as possible with everyone. We learn that the trader kept the Matabele from attacking the Barotse; that he prevented the Jesuits from getting a foothold in the country, not from prejudice but because of a promise he made Coillard; and that Coillard would have been unable to establish his stations without Westbeech's help, which was freely given because the latter wanted missionaries to blunt the savagery of the Africans in trans-Zambezia. His aid to Coillard is nowhere fully acknowledged by that missionary's editor or biographer, and it is time that Joros had his due. He was no saint, as he himself admits, but an effective man who made his living among barbarians and at the same time rendered them good service in other ways than simply by providing goods.

The diary is also a record of the last and fatal illness of its author. Disease of the liver, not his old enemy fever, seems to have killed him. Westbeech was '. . . careless of his health, and often reckless in his habits',[1] for he was a hard drinker and loved a session with his fellow interior men when the brandy arrived from Shoshong or Tati. His movements after the entries end can be traced. He set out for the Transvaal and was at Shoshong with his wagons, which were loaded with ivory, feathers, and skins, in late June or early July 1888. There he met a party of concession hunters bound for Matabeleland, and he gave them a letter of introduction to Lobengula and a gift of crane feathers for that chief. Westbeech died at Kalkfontein, Transvaal, on 17 July 1888 and

[1] George Lacy in *South Africa* magazine (London), 1895, p. 596.

was buried in the cemetery of the Jesuit mission at Vleeschfontein in the vicinity. He never reached home, though from another point of view his home was among the Barotse.

VII

The first notice the editor had of the existence of a diary by Westbeech was in a book catalogue. Messrs. Francis Edwards, Ltd., of London advertised for £25 a typed and bound copy as Item 680 in Catalogue No. 679, 1946. The volume was from the library of the late Sir Robert Coryndon, who was successively secretary to Cecil Rhodes, Administrator of North-Western Rhodesia for the British South Africa Company, High Commissioner for Zanzibar, and Governor of Kenya. The date of acquisition was 1903, and presumably, because of his interest in Barotse history, someone lent Westbeech's diary for copying while Coryndon was in Northern Rhodesia. The original typescript was given to the Rhodes-Livingstone Museum by Lady Coryndon some years ago, and it has been copied and circulated to interested persons.

Westbeech wrote as if he were addressing someone in particular, perhaps his wife. Holub implies[1] that the trader was keeping a journal in 1875–1876, but it may have been a ledger that the blank paper was taken from. On the other hand, diary keeping was a Victorian habit, and the discovery of an earlier record by Westbeech would be of great value to Rhodesian history. Attempts have been made to trace descendants and relatives in Southern Africa and England, so far without success.

VIII

Westbeech's highway in the Barotse country was the *Zambezi River*, a broad, shallow stream with vegetation-lined banks and many islands and rapids. Its length of about 265 miles from the mouth of the Chobe to Lealui was navigated in native dugout canoes, and the services of skilled African boatmen were available, at the orders of the King or the headmen if necessary. Difficult terrain and the presence of tsetse fly barred the ox wagon (Coil-

---

[1] *Seven Years in South Africa*, Vol. II, p. 255.

lard's taking of wagons to Sefula was a *tour de force*) from a large area north of the Zambezi, so the river was naturally the chief artery of trade and communication. All of the Barotse country, and especially the river valleys, was a malarial hell-hole in the wet summer season, and even in winter there were deaths among Europeans from this cause.

From the gateway, which was Impalera Village till 1877 and then Mambova Kraal till the building of Kazungula, the traveller was poled or paddled upstream past the Mambova Rapids (never a great obstacle) to New Sesheke, the centre of government for the Masubia tribe. At Mambova the river widens and passes through the Simalaha Flats, a distance of ninety miles. Two days' journey above Sesheke was Katonga or Sikhosi's, the last Masubia town, and eight miles beyond it lay the Katima Mulilo Rapids, the first of a series of twenty-four such obstructions in the seventy-five-mile stretch of river to Sioma. The first of these, Katima, was easily traversed, and at intervals of two miles and then seven miles above were the Mosila Ndimba and the Manyekanza rapids ; next in order came the Nambire, where one had to make a short portage, the Lusu (Death), the Bumbui, and the Kali. Matome Island was below the mouth of the Lumbe River, and then the small Nangura Fall and the Sitamba Rapids were surmounted to the Gonye Falls, the biggest of all, where canoes and goods were carried round for two miles and a half. The kraal of Sioma was about a mile above the Gonye, and a day's journey beyond the town began the wide, flat Barotse Valley or Barotse Plain, which extends past Lealui. The Zambezi was now free of major obstructions for a long distance, and the population was comparatively dense throughout this fertile region. The next town of importance was Nalolo, the residence of the King's sister, the Mukwae, on the right bank, and at last one came to Lealui, the Barotse capital.

IX

Four years after Westbeech opened Barotseland to Europeans from the south, two Scots, Norman Magnus MacLeod and William Frederic Fairlie, travelled north from Natal to see the Victoria Falls and to shoot big game. In rugged Victorian times the journey was not one for the ordinary tourist, but it was becoming increasingly popular with British young men of ample means and leisure. These two friends had been fellow officers in the 74th Highlanders, and they had as a companion Richard Cowley, a young Englishman living in Natal. MacLeod was the diarist and Fairlie the artist during their adventurous and in some ways disastrous journey of fifteen months.

MacLeod, the eldest son of Norman MacLeod of Dunvegan Castle, Isle of Skye, and Louisa, daughter of the thirteenth Baron St. John of Bletsoe, was born 27 July 1839 and was educated at Harrow. He was commissioned ensign without purchase in the 74th Foot on 31 March 1858 and became lieutenant by purchase on 16 October 1860. He served as aide-de-camp to General Sir Hope Grant, Commander in Chief at Madras, from 1863 to 1865, and during his tour of duty in India[1] he visited the Andaman Islands and Burma. MacLeod left Madras for home early in June 1865, and from July 1865 to February 1868 he served with his regiment in England and Ireland and became captain by purchase on 9 March 1867. His next tour of duty abroad was at Gibraltar, February 1868 to March 1872, with excursions to North Africa and Spain and leaves at Dunvegan and in England. Fairlie served at Gibraltar also, and the two officers must have renewed and strengthened their friendship at that fortress. Upon transfer to Malta, MacLeod, apparently weary of garrison duty, submitted his resignation from the Army in September 1872 (it was effective on the first of January following) and went to Albania to hunt from November to January 1873.

MacLeod, in England again in February, soon embarked on the most interesting and important part of his life, the years spent in South Africa. He left Southampton early in June in a vessel of the Union Company and, after a few days at Cape Town and a change of ships, he arrived at Durban on 16 July. W. F. Fairlie and his brother Reginald had come there from home about a

[1] During 1864 MacLeod made two shikar trips with Lieutenant Henry Faulkner, 17th Lancers, who later was an explorer and hunter in Nyasaland.

month before, and the three of them soon started for Zululand to
hunt and to attend Cetshwayo's coronation. Theophilus Shepstone, Secretary for Native Affairs for Natal, and his large escort
overtook them on the road, and the coronation was held at the
royal kraal on 1 September. MacLeod wrote an interesting description of the event, and both he and W. Fairlie left diaries of
their Zululand journey. The three sportsmen, with John Dunn's
permission and help and accompanied by an old hunter named
Lewis Reynolds, made a shooting trip on foot in the country
between the Black and White Umfolozi rivers for the rest of the
month.

MacLeod proceeded to Pietermaritzburg, where he hired his
wagon to the Government to transport 4,500 pounds of arms and
ammunition to the forces operating against Langalibalele. With six
other wagons and a military escort he trekked in November to
Bushman's Pass, where his party buried the neglected dead of the
brush with the rebel chief's people. MacLeod wanted to go to the
Transvaal Goldfields, where the Fairlies had gone, but instead he
accepted an offer by the Natal Government of a trip to India as
Special Agent for Coolie Immigration, at £50 per month and ex-
penses. He toured the sugar plantations in December to inquire
into labour requirements and sailed for Zanzibar on 6 January
1874.

From Zanzibar he voyaged to Kilwa in a dhow taking supplies
to J. F. Elton, an agent for the suppression of the slave trade in
East Africa. MacLeod left Zanzibar again early in February for
Calcutta where, finding that a temporary agent for emigration to
Natal had been appointed, he agreed to let the appointment become permanent. He travelled in the north of India and in June
embarked in a coolie ship that reached Durban on 8 July, but
those on board passed the next eighteen days in quarantine, owing
to an outbreak of cholera in the vessel. The Lieutenant-Governor
commended MacLeod to the Legislative Council for the manner
in which his mission was conducted.

The ex-captain lived at Maritzburg, from which he travelled
and hunted, for the next six months. From 1 October 1874 he

served three months as Protector of Immigrants, an office that carried with it membership on the Executive and Legislative Councils. He succeeded J. F. Elton and was relieved of his duties by H. C. Shepstone. Fairlie returned to Maritzburg from the Transvaal about November, and he and MacLeod prepared for their trip to the Zambezi during the next two months. They left the town on 7 February 1875 and returned to it on 16 May 1876.

On the 30th of June following, MacLeod sailed from Durban for England, where he arrived a month later. He passed the remainder of the year and all of 1877 in Britain and on the Continent. He and Fairlie planned to meet in Ceylon to hunt, but MacLeod thought South Africa better for that, so he wired Fairlie to meet him there. MacLeod left England in March 1878 and reached Durban on 21 April, to find that his friend had missed his telegram at Aden and had gone to Quelimane with Herbert Rhodes to hunt on the Shire River and about Lake Nyasa. MacLeod waited, and Fairlie came to Natal ill with malaria after having been up the Zambezi to Shupanga. The two men stayed at Maritzburg, and between 7 September and 4 October Fairlie journeyed to Quelimane and back to fetch his kit.

In view of impending war with the Zulus, Sir Bartle Frere appointed MacLeod Civil and Political Assistant to the Officer Commanding at Utrecht (Colonel Evelyn Wood) and Border Agent to the Swazis, at a salary of £500 per year. He was also made a justice of the peace for the districts of Utrecht, Wakkerstroom, and Lydenburg, this commission bearing the date 22 November 1878. Fairlie also went to the Transvaal, to be commandant of a police force of 200 men, his salary to be £1 per day. MacLeod was to prevent the Swazis from joining the Zulus, to enlist their active aid if possible, and to raise the police force from among them. These appointments were made about the middle of October 1878, and on the 22nd of that month they left Maritzburg for Utrecht, where they reported to Wood and then rode 150 miles to the kraal of Umbandine, the Swazi king. MacLeod's first interview with that potentate took place on 12 November.

The two friends lived at Derby, a hamlet of five houses and a

store built in the Transvaal on the Swazi border by McCorkin-
dale, promoter of the New Scotland settlement scheme. MacLeod
had to travel a good deal in all kinds of weather, and his tasks were
numerous and varied. He successfully managed the Swazis, distri-
buted or returned captured Zulu cattle, looked after Zulu refugees,
dealt with a few whites who took advantage of the situation to steal
Swazi cattle, and fended off several incompetent and meddling
British officers. The local Boers refused to serve under Wood and
most of them trekked away, though a few who remained went to
Zululand and conspired with Cetshwayo. To add to the confusion,
there were many rumours of impending attacks by Zulu impis,
who did make the roads in the area unsafe. However, things became easier in March 1879 with the surrender to MacLeod of
Ohamo, Cetshwayo's brother and the second most important
Zulu, and after Ulundi all danger was gone.

Arthur Neumann, later famous as an elephant hunter in East
Africa, served as MacLeod's interpreter and as an officer in Fairlie's Swazi Police. That force made some small raids into Zululand, but it was disbanded as useless on MacLeod's recommenda-
tion and was paid off on 20 April. Fairlie left Derby to find another
commission, and Neumann left in July.

The Swazis wanted to see the Zulus beaten because they dis-
liked and feared them, but the Swazis thought the British unable
to win the war and so at first preferred to wait and watch events.
They were never used against the Zulus because they would not
move unless supported by a large British force. Umbandine called
up his army at MacLeod's request in July, but the agent refused
to let it move into Zululand—the enemy was beaten and the
Swazis would only murder and plunder. MacLeod with another
native force took part in the final pacification from the Transvaal
side.

Sir Garnet Wolseley ordered MacLeod, on 30 October 1879,
to gather and march a Swazi army to fight Sekukuni. The agent
rushed to the King's kraal, where 8,000 warriors were rapidly
mobilized, and he left with them on 9 November. They marched
via Lydenburg, Fort Jellabad, and Fort Burgers to Sekukuni's

Mountain, and at daylight on 28 November they stormed the pass on one side and cleared the caves with much hard fighting. MacLeod led his native army home by 17 December, after it fought in the hills for a few more days. Only he could have prevailed on them to go, for the Swazis believed in and trusted him. They behaved and fought well, had over 500 men killed and many wounded, and took about 5,000 cattle.

MacLeod stayed on at Derby to help a commission instructed to settle and beacon the boundary between the Transvaal and Swaziland, and on 15 March 1880 his duties were taken over by Sir Morrison Barlow. He proceeded to Natal, left Durban for home on 6 April, and was in England early in May. He was mentioned in Lord Chelmsford's dispatches for his services during the Zulu War. In 1881 MacLeod married Emily Caroline, daughter of Sir Charles Isham of Lampost Hall, Northamptonshire, and he became the 26th Chief of the Clan MacLeod of MacLeod and the owner of 82,000 acres. He served in various capacities in Scotland and died 5 November 1929, survived by one daughter.

MacLeod's career in India and South Africa is recorded in his summary diary for 1863–1880, a manuscript volume of 92 leaves bound in half leather and with his bookplate. This book of ruled blue paper measures $12\frac{3}{4} \times 8$ inches, and in it are pasted racing programmes and newspaper clippings. The short account of his journey to the Zambezi that is printed herein is a part of this diary.

X

William Frederic Fairlie was the son of James Ogilvy Fairlie (1809–1870) of Coodham, Ayrshire, who was once lieutenant and captain in the 2nd Life Guards and later was lieutenant-colonel commanding the Ayrshire Yeomanry Cavalry. The father had a son and daughter by his first wife and seven children, including William Frederic and Reginald Norman (1850–1913) by his second, Elizabeth Craufurd of Craufurland, Ayrshire.

Fairlie was born 5 January 1847 and was educated at Glenalmond in Perthshire. He became ensign in the 9th Foot by purchase on 13 February 1867, exchanged into the 74th Foot on the same date, and became lieutenant by purchase on 27 November 1867. Fairlie and MacLeod, whose families were connected by marriage, were great friends, and the former probably exchanged into the 74th Highlanders to be with MacLeod. They travelled and served together for many years. While in garrison at Gibraltar in 1871, they accompanied Colonel Matthews, United States Consul General at Tangier, on an official visit to the Emperor of Morocco, and Fairlie left an account of their journey. He retired from the Army and received the value of his commission on 26 March 1873, in order to go adventuring in Africa with MacLeod. They were tired of garrison life, though it seems to have been unconfining for officers.

After the voyage to Natal and the trip to Zululand, Fairlie and his brother Reginald went shooting in the eastern Transvaal and Swaziland from Lydenburg in the winter of 1874. They returned to Natal about November, and Reginald apparently went home, while his brother and MacLeod stayed behind to prepare for their long journey to the Zambezi and Barotseland. Fairlie visited Ceylon, where his family had tea-planting interests, in 1877, and he ascended the Zambezi to Shupanga in September 1878. He returned to Natal to serve with MacLeod in the Transvaal, where Fairlie's Swazi Police were raised to a strength of about a hundred men by mid-January 1879. That force patrolled the Zulu border till its disbandment, soon after which Fairlie left Derby for Wood's headquarters. He served at the Battle of Ulundi with Wood's Column, apparently as a member of the Natal Police, which was formed in 1874 under Major John Dartnell and existed until amalgamated with other forces in 1913.

Early in 1880 Fairlie was trying to obtain an inspectorship in the Natal Police, but, failing to get it, he went elephant hunting to the west of the upper Shire River. Next year he spent four months shooting elephants at the north end of Lake Nyasa with two companions, one of whom may have been MacLeod and the other Lieutenant Henry Faulkner.

Fairlie married in 1885 May, the daughter of Peter Paterson of Renfrew House, Estcourt, Natal, a civil engineer and later a judge of the High Court. The couple had two daughters. Fairlie joined the Natal Police and during the South African War commanded the Zululand Native Police (Nonggai) with eight European officers and 800 men. In the Zululand Rebellion of 1906 he served as commander of a hundred of these men, who did good work and were disbanded at its close. Fairlie returned to Great Britain soon after and died there 12 October 1923.

Fairlie was a quiet and unassuming man, a good soldier and leader, and a first-rate sportsman. He had a great sense of humour and, as his sketches show, he was a competent, though untaught, artist. His sketchbook, which has been preserved by a daughter, is a blank book bound in half leather, much battered and with many leaves loose. The paper measures $10\frac{3}{4} \times 8\frac{5}{8}$ inches, and on the front flyleaf is written 'W. F. Fairlie, May 1876', and on the verso of this leaf, 'From Natal to the Zambesi—1875-76'. There are 115 sketches made by W. F. Fairlie on his journey to the Zambezi and in Barotseland, though a few of these are of game near Delagoa Bay and in Nyasaland; 12 sketches done by Reginald Fairlie in Swaziland; and 24 pictures made in Ceylon by W. F. Fairlie. They are in pencil, in pen and ink, and in pen and ink coloured with watercolour. They are on a variety of papers different from that of the book and are mounted or pasted, one, two, or three to a leaf, on the rectos; some are attached to versos, and others are pasted to the stubs of numerous leaves that have been cut out. W. F. Fairlie's African sketches have been numbered consecutively by the editor, and these numbers are used for those sketches reproduced in this book. The captions are the artist's.

XI

The editor is indebted to many persons for their friendly and helpful co-operation in the making of this book. Lady Coryndon has kindly given permission for the publication of George Westbeech's diary. Dame Flora MacLeod of Dunvegan Castle, Isle of Skye, lent the 26th Chief's diary and papers for copying, furnished photographs of him, and gave permission to publish. Her daugh-

ter, Mrs. Joan Gordon, efficiently aided us in all of this. Mrs. C.
M. Forwood of Beaumont, Jersey, Channel Isles, lent her father's
sketchbook and gave information about him and copies of his
journals and articles; she also kindly consented to the publication
of his sketches. Mr. J. O. Fairlie of Myres Castle, Auchter-
muchty, Fifeshire, sent facts about the life of his relative W. F.
Fairlie.

Mr. Robert D. Brumley of South Charleston, West Virginia,
U.S.A., generously gave his time and skill to the photographic
copying of the Fairlie pictures.

Others who made substantial contributions from their know-
ledge and experience are: Dr. and Mrs. J. Desmond Clark of the
Rhodes-Livingstone Museum; Mr. D. W. King, Librarian of
the War Office, London; Messrs. W. T. Baxter and E. E. Burke,
National Archives of Rhodesia and Nyasaland, Salisbury; The
Surveyor General of the Federation and his department; Mr.
Piers Raymond of Chatto and Windus, London; Mr. F. M.
Merifield, District Officer at Sesheke; Mr. Wium, Magistrate of
the Eastern Caprivi Zipfel; Mrs. Kenneth Bourne of Charleston,
West Virginia, U.S.A.; and Mr. Gervas Clay of the Rhodes-
Livingstone Museum.

No. 5

Our Waggons. 25th Feb. 1875

The ox wagon was the usual means of travel and freighting in Southern Africa, and his wagon served the interior traveller as a peripatetic home and storehouse and sometimes as a fort. These are full-tented wagons, and they are shown with the trektows extended and the yokes attached. The after oxen were yoked to the wagon pole or disselboom, and the rest of the span to its extension, the trektow or 'pull rope,' which was a chain or a rope made of strips of prepared hide. The yoke skeys or yoke pins, between the pairs of which the necks of the oxen were fastened by throat straps, are shown in the yokes. By counting yokes, it can be seen that the wagon on the right was drawn by a span of twelve bullocks ; fourteen or sixteen were more common at the time in the interior. This vehicle has been rigged with a tarpaulin or tent to give added protection from the weather during the halt.

No. 30

The Chief–Bamangwato. Kama

Khama (Hartebeest), chief of the Mangwato tribe of the Bechuana group, is shown in European clothes and seated on a camp chair inside the *kxotla*, the palisaded meeting and council arena. The capital of this tribe was the town of Shoshong, sometimes called Bamangwato after its people. Khama (? 1828–1923) was the greatest chief of the Mangwato, and he was a sincere Christian from his baptism by a German missionary in 1860. He ruled 1872–1873 and 1875–1923. As a result of his influence and the labours of missionaries, some of his people were Christians and were partly Europeanized by this time.

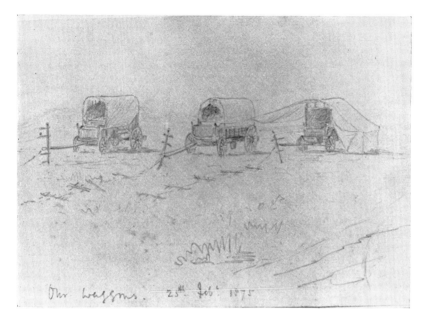

Our waggons. 25th Feb: 1875

No. 5

No. 30

Women at Bamangwato.

13th April 187

No. 31

No. 32

No. 31

Women at Bamangwato. 15th April 1875

Showing two women attired in karosses; cloaks made of prepared hide or of furs. One of them carries a baby in typical African fashion, and the bracelets, anklets, and necklaces are made of beads, an important article of trade. The coiffures of the two who are standing are not typically Central African, and they look as if they are wearing wigs such as are found among some South-West African peoples. The triangles in the middle distance are the huts of Shoshong, which stood at the mouth of a gorge in the bare, basaltic Mangwato Hills of the background.

No. 32

Stalking a Wildebeest. Kari Kari. 3rd May 1875

Fairlie and his friends were sportsmen, though the game they killed was not wasted. African servants loved meat and expected white men to provide plenty of it. Meat kept them happy. Besides, a wagon could not be loaded with enough grain and tinned food to feed even a small party during so long a journey in the wilderness. The locale is the eastern edge of the Makarikari Salt Pan, a huge depression into which some of the drainage from the Okavango Swamps finds its way, to evaporate in the dry or winter season. Cover is scant, and the wildebeest looks very much on the *qui vive*.

The Diary of
George Westbeech
1885–1888

THE DIARY OF GEORGE WESTBEECH
1885–1888

HAVING left Bamangwato[1] on the 20th March '85 after delaying to get some sheep by the way, arrived at Maghalapsie[2] on the 23rd, where we had a lively stick fast for four hours; after, however, as Geo. Hall[3] calls it 'double banking'[4] we got out. Passed Touani and Chackani Vleis,[5] where ten ducks were bagged, also passed a poor foot-sore Englishman, who about six weeks ago went to Tati on foot to look for work, and was now returning utterly exhausted, with clothes and blankets strapped to his back, a small kettle of drink water in hand, and, poor fellow, nothing to eat. Well, that he soon got in the way of a quarter of mutton, and he went on his way rejoicing and so did we.

Game very scarce, not even a stein buck spoor; wolves[6] are, however, plentiful, but they not being considered by such an epicure (?) as myself, dainties, are no use even trying to shoot to keep the pot boiling. Band of hind wheel came off six miles from Matlousia.[7] Having nothing to repair it [with], left the driver in

[1] Shoshong, a large native town and capital of the Mangwato tribe. See sketches 30 and 31. This was the point of departure for the farthest interior–the Zambezi country, Ngamiland, Matabeleland, and Mashonaland.

[2] The Mhlapshwe River, a periodic or sand river twenty-five miles from Shoshong on the road to Matabeleland. It was dry in winter but held water a little way under the sand in its bed.

[3] George Hall was an American who came to South Africa to work for Cobb and Company, a transport service that operated between Port Elizabeth and the Diamond Fields. He found his way to the Tati Goldfields in 1871 and worked and lived there till about 1888.

[4] Double teaming, or hitching a second span of oxen to the first to pull a wagon out of a bad place. The drifts or fords of sand rivers usually had steep banks and their beds were full of deep sand, both difficult to get wagons over.

[5] The Towani River, another dry stream bed and permanent water, eleven or twelve miles from the Mhlapshwe. Chakane Pan, ten miles from Towani, a pool west of the Mokoro Hills that held water till the end of winter, sometimes till November.

[6] Spotted hyenas.

[7] The Maklautsi River, a large tributary of the Limpopo, was dry in winter. The road crossed it twenty-eight miles south of Tati.

THE DIARY OF GEORGE WESTBEECH

March, 1885

charge and started for Tati.[1] Arrived at that place, got a wheel
which I sent with the boys to the broken-down wagon, which fit-
ting, the wagon turned up after four days delay. It then took six
days more before I could get wagon repaired, which being done,
however, at last I started (but not before nearly breaking my hip
and three ribs, my horse having come down on the stones) for
Mangwe.[2] Arrived and stayed two days there, putting things
square, and started on horseback for Gubulawayo,[3] which place I
reached on the second day, quietly dismounted, and found Philips,
Fairbairn[4] and a few others quietly ruminating on their former
happy lives, over a calabash of Kafir beer. Joined them, and proceeded with them to be dull and got dullest when I thought of the
past three months. However, as things change, thought they
might for us, so had another cup of juice and proceeded to dinner.

Next day rode to see Lobengula, the King,[5] and after doing all
I had to do with him, which, however, took me six days, said goodbye to Phil, Fairbairn and Collison,[6] and started back for the

[1] A small white settlement on the north bank of the Tati River, founded during the
first gold rush in South Africa, in 1868. The population dwindled rapidly after two
years, when it was seen that working the hard quartz ore was uneconomical, but gold
continued to be mined intermittently in small quantities during the 1870's and
1880's. Permanent white residents were very few in number. Tati was a base for
travel to Matabeleland and the Zambezi; the Westbeech Road began there and linked
Tati to the shorter road to the Zambezi from Shoshong via the Makarikari Salt Pan.

[2] The Mangwe River, a perennial stream crossed near its headwaters. The elephant hunter John Lee lived there on a farm granted him by Mzilikazi, the first
Matabele king. Lee's was another refreshment station on the way to the Matabele
country.

[3] New Bulawayo, capital or chief town of the Matabele people. It was built round
the King's kraal, which was at or near the site of Government House in European
Bulawayo. Moved from an earlier first site in 1881, it existed till it was destroyed in
the Matabele War of 1893.

[4] 'Elephant' Phillips, Westbeech's partner and the Matabeleland representative in
their trading enterprises. James Fairbairn was a Scots trader who first came to Matabeleland in 1872 and died at Inyati in 1894. He became a fixture in the country,
built up a large business, and won Lobengula's confidence.

[5] Lobengula (? 1836–1893), second and last King of the Matabele and an old
friend of Westbeech's. As a young man, and before he became the ruler, he travelled
and hunted with Westbeech and Phillips.

[6] H. C. Collison, a trader and hunter from Norfolk, is first recorded in the interior
during 1877, at the Zambezi; he was at the Chobe River in 1879 and with Selous in
Mashonaland in 1880 and 1883. He died at Kimberley Hospital in 1888.

26

May, 1885

wagons. Got to them, found everything all serene and started on a new road[1] for the Zambesi road, which turns out to be about seven days further than the old road via Tati.

Not been able to get a single thing to shoot at up to the present, viz. 21st May. However, on that night shot a wolf, and next morning at Jurua[2] a giraffe, which was a God-send, as I for one was getting tired of sardines (sprats) and pap.[3] Dried the meat, and whilst on giraffe spoor again, a Bushman, who had diverged, got fresh elephant spoor, followed it without letting us know, and next morning, behold, he appears with a foot, a piece of trunk and the tail. He had caught up to the troop, and a big troop they were, and shot a cow. Well, after expressing my anger and hurting my hand doing so, I had a hole dug and washed the trunk and foot, which after being cooked and allowed to cool, we began with the aid of Lea & Perrins to dissect. And it went down *well*.

Perhaps you for whom I'm writing all this trip's doings might not appreciate our veldt cuisine ; still those two articles are thought lots of by old interior men. With the meat we began to fatten up our dogs and boys, which was only an affair of a few days ; for the role used to be, herds about 20 pounds of meat, with the cattle to the veldt, there to fill up. Wagon boys cram as much as they could and sleep, then wake up, cram again and return to Morpheus and an occasional greasing of the outer man until they began to shine. Dogs same law as Kafirs, feed until they couldn't manage any more, then sleep. Well, as soon as my meat was dry, inspanned and proceeded for Panda Matinga,[4] where we arrived on the 28th

[1] Impossible to identify from this. During the preceding decade there was a road or track passable for wagons from Old Bulawayo, west over the Khami and Gwaai rivers, to the Nata River, and down it or paralleling its course, to Nwasha or other permanent waters on the Zambezi Road.

[2] Gerufa, the next permanent watering place north of Nwasha Pan on the Zambezi Road.

[3] Porridge, made of ground mealies or kaffir corn by stirring handfuls of the coarse meal into boiling water until a stiff cooked mass was obtained.

[4] Pandamatenga, a hamlet and trading station on a hillock overlooking the most southerly of the headstreams of the Matetsi River, was established by Westbeech himself soon after 1871 as a headquarters for his trade into Barotseland. It was a rendezvous for Europeans for many years and the only settlement of whites and half-

May and found everything all serene, but trade very bad, the country of the Barotse being very unsettled, and civil war going on in the valley. It appears that they had driven their old chief, Leboche,[1] away and had appointed another, named Wa-ga-Funa, in his stead ; who immediately, to get power, began killing all who were adverse to him, and now nearly all my old friends of Sepopa's [time] are either killed or driven away. Those who have escaped have gone to try and find Leboche, and one old chief, M'wala, who was a great friend of mine and the King's trading induna, has taken possession of a large island in the Zambesi with all his people who have stuck to him, and prevents Wa-ga-Funa's boats from either going up or down the river. How things will turn out, don't know.[2] So ends May.

June 6th. Started on horseback for Leshuma,[3] my last advanced point of civilisation near the Zambesi where I have a store. Arrived on the 7th and found everything very quiet, far too much so, for there was also no trade doing. Heard there that affairs could not be worse than they were across the river.

Met an old Marotse friend who was returning to the valley and sent by him a message to the King, advising him of my arrival in the country.

Saw also Coillard,[4] the missionary, who although the country is

castes northwest of Tati. The Matetsi was during that period the terminus of wagon travel in the direction of the Zambezi because tsetse fly barred the way beyond. Towards the end of his life, Westbeech was able to move his storehouses to the river, as is mentioned in this diary, owing to the retreat of the fly.

[1] Lubosi or Robosi, who afterwards took the name *Lewanika*. The new king appointed in his stead was his cousin, Akufuna Tatila. It was common enough for a Lozi to have two names.

[2] The rising against Lewanika occurred in July 1884.

[3] A watering place in the Lesuma Valley and eleven miles south of the Chobe-Zambezi junction. As early as 1878 Westbeech and Phillips had a collection of huts there for storehouses and living quarters and were using it as an advanced base. Wagons could be brought there and returned to Pandamatenga under cover of darkness, when the tsetse fly was inactive.

[4] The Rev. François Coillard (1834–1904), of the *Société des Missions Evangéliques de Paris*, a Protestant missionary body. He and his party arrived at Lesuma on 26 July 1884 and maintained a base camp there until they, with the help of the Africans, took their wagons across the Zambezi in August 1885. It is this move towards permanently establishing themselves in Barotseland to which Westbeech refers.

June–July, 1885

so disturbed and against my advice, persists nevertheless in making ready to go through. Left Leshoma on the 12th for Panda Matenga.

After being there a few days, saw a wagon coming down the valley, which turned out to be Messrs. Scott, Inman and Brock[1] to see the Falls and get a little hunting. After being a few days here and finding them jolly people, as they could not get a guide to the Falls went with them in that capacity and a jolly trip we had. They enjoyed themselves thoroughly and so did I. Were away ten days and then returned here and as they then wished to return to civilisation and I was sending wagons out to Klerksdorp they took advantage of my boy's knowledge of the country to travel at the same time [as he] and left here on the 21st July all well.

Quiet after their exodus for a few days, but on the 27th Harry Ware[2] arrived, having brought a gentleman from England to also see the Falls and hunt (a Mr. Reid). Harry had broken his thigh on the Nata River whilst hunting, his horse having fallen on top of him ; however, the leg was re-set and was doing well, though he could not walk without crutches, so had him carried from his wagon up to my house and looked after him, he being an old friend of mine. I took all Reid's affairs into my own hands, got boys to take him to the Falls, and as I had occasion to go to Leshoma to see some native head men, told Reid that I would meet him at that place ; which I did and got him hunting veldt across the Zambesi in my hunting country.[3]

[1] British sportsmen not further identified. Scott came up partly for his health and had a satisfactory trip. As early as 1863 British travellers were going upcountry to see the Victoria Falls and to hunt, a journey not then recommended for the ordinary tourist.

[2] Harry Ware was a trader who by 1885 had been several years in Africa and had made three journeys to the Zambezi. He advertized in *The Field* newspaper that he would conduct sportsmen to the Victoria Falls, and Percy C. Reid, an ex-officer of the 15th Hussars and nephew to Sir Henry Barkly (onetime Governor of the Cape), became his client. Ware broke his thigh on 9 June, and Reid and two boys set it, but the leg became shorter than the other. Reid was again at the Zambezi in 1888, 1895, and 1899, and Ware conducted him and a Mr. and Mrs. Thomas there in 1888. In 1889 Ware, representing a mining syndicate, obtained from Lewanika a mineral concession to the Batoka country, from the Machili River to the borders of the Mashukulumbwe (BaIla). It was sold to Kimberley business men, who in turn sold it to Rhodes for the Chartered Company.

[3] He obtained permission, probably from the headmen at Sesheke, for Reid to hunt in a specified area. Westbeech's permanent hunting veld was the valley of the Machili River.

Saw the headmen, sent another message to the Barotse, and returned to Panda Matenga. Had not been long at home before I got a message that the chief M'wala had left his island and after killing three headmen opposed to the deposed King, fled through the Chobe to join Leboche; and that the Barotse country was very unsettled.

On the 30th August Reid returned, having had a very successful hunt and killed all he wanted, except an elephant and lion. The former he did not come across, but of the latter he saw seven, though he could not get a shot at them.

On the 2nd September received another message that Leboche was returned through the Zambesi with many people and was still collecting at the Gonye Falls; that the new chief had fled to the country from whence he came and that the headmen were collecting soldiers to oppose Leboche, but many people were bolting; that the Shesheki indunas refused to assist in expelling Leboche, as they had not been called to assist when he was driven out last year; that the messenger I had sent to the Barotse had returned to Shesheki, having under existing circumstances been afraid to go on. Also that Coillard is through the river with wife, bag and baggage, and insists upon pushing on.[1] Well, he must e'en his ain gait (is that Scotch?).

Ware and Reid started on the 3rd on their return south, Harry still on crutches, his oxen miserably poor, in fact, I don't think he will get far, although I have lent him two and the Jesuits[2] have sold him two, but Reid is anxious to get back to England and Harry is bound to do his best to get him out.

5th Sept. My birthday. Went into the sheep kraal to try if I

[1] Coillard and his party reached Sesheke with their wagons on 24 September. The mission station at that town, in charge of Jeanmairet, was founded then. Farther advance was held up by rain, lack of a road, and the internal strife in Barotseland.

[2] The first Jesuit mission came to the interior in 1879, led by Father Depelchin, and a station was established at Old Bulawayo. It was the intention to work in the Zambezi Valley, and next winter Depelchin, with two other priests and two brothers, made a reconnaissance to the Victoria Falls and the Batoka country. A station was initiated at Pandamatenga. By 1885 Fathers Kroot and Booms and Brothers De Sadeleer, Allen, and Vervenne were there. Allen died there of fever on 2 February 1885, and Kroot, who was ill, was taken by Booms to Old Bulawayo, where he died on 21 June.

September, 1885

couldn't get a bit of mutton instead of continually eating game ; but all that I put my hand over was just skin and bone, so sighed, went back to the house, made a plum pudding, fried sable antelope steak with onions, and sat down to a fashionable 7 P.M. dinner and opened a bottle of whisky, which myself and a young man who came from Klerksdorp with me and is now in my employ (W. Horn)[1] enjoyed.

On the 7th two boys arrived from H. Ware driving on two very poor oxen (one of them being his front ox) with a letter to me asking Dear George to please look after them and if they live he shall only be too glad. Started his boys back with the assurance that Dear George would do his best, and started to feed his two oxen with green barley which I had planted for my horse.

12th. Two of my boys returned from across the Zambesi having shot seven elephants. They say that elephants are plentiful, but it is so far that they want me to go with them, as the Kafirs all know me for the last fifteen years, and then they can hunt well, but alone they don't care about going ; so as soon as my wagon returns from Bamangwato I shall collect all my hunters and go with them hunting for six months for the Barotse are so unsettled that there will be nothing done with them for a long time as none of them are now hunting for ivory, but waiting to see how affairs will go in the valley.

On the 15th, Harry's front ox died ; the other may pull through. I've sent it away to better veldt.

26th. Dr. and Mrs. Holub[2] with party arrived here, having had

[1] A trader named W. Horn was at the Zambezi in 1868, when he attempted to do business with the Barotse. He came away disgusted with his treatment and thereafter preferred to trade with the Matabele. If this man was young, he may have been the son of the W. Horn of the 1860's and 1870's.

[2] Emil Holub (1847–1902), a Czech doctor of medicine from Prague, first came to South Africa in 1872. From boyhood African exploration had been his goal and Livingstone his ideal. He practiced at the Diamond Fields, in order to get money for equipping himself, and made journeys to the Transvaal and to Shoshong to learn about travel. In 1875, with one companion, Holub arrived at the Zambezi with the object of following Livingstone's footsteps to Angola and the west coast. Although helped by Westbeech and Sipopa, he failed to ascend the Zambezi very far, because of illness and lack of means. He returned in 1880 to Europe, where he made a reputation as an explorer by writing and exhibiting his extensive collections. This was his second attempt to penetrate beyond the Zambezi, and this time he had a large and well-equipped expedition.

31

to leave two of their wagons behind as thirty-two oxen had died from eating poison.[1] That and other severe losses they have had, has induced me to be of any assistance that I can to them, and try and get them through the Zambesi. Their mission is to Lake Bangweolo, from thence to Tanganyika, and so to the Congo. I really do not think they will succeed. Perhaps they may, but it will be with great difficulty and at much expense. Heard that the deposed chief Leboche is again through the Zambesi with a pretty good force and seems determined to win back his country. Hope he may. The new chief, Wa-ga-Funa, has fled; all the Mamboo-wa[2] people are fled to the island, Leboche having already entered the Barotse Valley.

October 4th. Gave Dr. H. one of my hunters as a guide to the Falls. On the 5th, two of the Dr.'s men following game lost themselves and did not turn up at Panda Matenga until the night of the 8th, very hungry and foot-sore. They had expended all their cartridges firing signal shots, so having none left to get game with, got none, nor could they even catch frogs. However, as they stuck to the Daika[3] tributaries they had plenty of water, so it was not so bad. The Dr. and party started on the 9th for the Falls, and I heard that the Shesheki party were divided, those for Leboche having crossed the Zambesi for the Linyanti[4] side, and the Wa-ga-Funa party gone amongst the Matotela tribe.[5]

[1] Or tulp, plants poisonous to animals and of the genera *Moraea* and *Homeria*. The active principal is the alkaloid homeridine.

[2] Mambova, the village of the headman Makumba, was, after the desertion of Impalera Village during the civil war that resulted in the ousting of Mwanawina, the gateway to Barotseland. It was situated on the left bank of the Zambezi about eight miles above the mouth of the Chobe, and in 1881 it had, with its neighbouring small kraals, a population of five or six hundred. 'The island' was perhaps Impalera, the land between the Chobe and the Zambezi rivers.

[3] The Deka River, a tributary of the Zambezi that enters the latter some sixty-five miles east of the Falls. Near its source the Deka was a standplace or halt for wagons on the Zambezi Road, the first one south of Pandamatenga.

[4] Linyanti or Dinyanti was the chief town of the Makololo overlords and the place where Livingstone first found them. It was on the north side of the Chobe River opposite the mouth of the Savuti Channel. The 'Linyanti side' would mean the country of the Chobe (sometimes called the Linyanti)–Kwando river system.

[5] The Matotela. See Introduction.

October, 1885

Coillard and party are at Shesheki, very lively they must have it. Thermometer 110, clouds thick, but, bad luck to them, they won't break and give us a little of their contents, which is much needed.

Night of the 13th, rain at last. Two mopani[1] trees struck by lightning in my yard. It was a terrific storm but did not last long.

17*th*. Leboche has fought and won and is again King ;[2] at all events, so says rumour. Shall be pleased if the news is confirmed, although it will take some months before the country will be settled.

29*th*. True it is. Five men came last night from Leshoma having been sent by their chief, who is sent by Leboche, to see me and ask me to go and meet him in the valley, for which place he is en route, having driven or caused to be driven out of the country, all who were against him. I shall start tomorrow for Leshoma, to interview those sent and hear their news.

Left on the 30th for Leshoma, where I arrived all serene but knocked up by the sun, as there was not a drop of water on the road, a distance of at least sixty miles. Saw the men sent to me by Leboche, from whom I received two tusks, a present. Heard all their news, gave them mine and they left to rejoin the King.

After they were gone some people arrived from Sheseki from the headman of that place, being sent on private mission to me in case he, Maransian,[3] should be forced to fly, whether if he came to

---

[1] The mopane (*Copaifera mopani*), a deciduous tree very common in the Rhodesias and the northern Bechuanaland Protectorate and west to Ovamboland. It grows from forty to fifty feet tall on deep soil and will live in ground that is seasonally flooded or in shallow or brack soil.

[2] Lewanika regained his chieftainship in October 1885, after a hard-fought battle near Lealui.

[3] Mulasiane (Maransian) was the title of the principal induna or headman of Sesheke. The office was filled at this time by one Sikabenga, who had succeeded his father, the incumbent in 1878. Sikabenga, a young man with a weak face, was related to Mataa, the most important rebel chief and partisan of Akafuna. The Mulasiane was anticipating Lewanika's vengeance, which came on 26 and 27 December 1885, when he was attacked the by King's people in Seseke. He escaped and took refuge with Siachitema, a petty Batoka chief who lived on the borders of the Mashukulumbwe.

33

me I would protect him. Of course I assured them that I would do as much for him as I did for Selumbu[1] in '75 who sought protection from Sepopa's tyranny with me, and I then proceeded to ask them the news, which is that no battle has been fought, no one has been driven out ; that Leboche is not en route for the valley, but in hiding either at Linyanti or Umtembanja's,[2] and that events may turn out that he may never regain the kingdom ; that the headmen of Shesheki, eleven in number, under the chief one, Maransian, who had sent them (the messengers) were divided. Some had fled to an island in the Zambesi and their people had left them, and others with all their people were with Maransian and his followers, a great number and well armed, at the gardens awaiting events ; but that if forced to flee he had sent to me to ask sanctuary of me, and now as they did and would return to their master, who has since sent to thank me.

Left Leshuma at 2 P.M. on the 6th and arrived here to breakfast on the 7th where everything has gone on smoothly, excepting that four of Dr. Holub's party are down with fever[3] and an Englishman, W. Horn, in my employ down with it also. I expect it will be pretty brisk (the fever) this year. We old stagers may sneak off lightly, but fresh unzambesi-ised bloods will get a little thinner this year.

Dr. H. and party returned from the Falls on the 6th, but have had to leave the iron wagonette with which they went, on the road, broken down, two wheels broken. They have, however, sent a tradesman to mend it, so it may soon be here.

12*th* and no wagon here but the man left at the broken wagonette and one of two sent are down with fever. One of my hunters has gone to shoot game for them, so that they can have some meat.

[1] Or Silumbu, Lewanika's Ngambela or Prime Minister in 1878.

[2] Matambanje, a superior sort of African then about fifty years old. He was a chief of the Mashi tribe whose village was on the left bank of the Kwando River above the Chobe swamps, at about 17° 10' south latitude. Lewanika and his partisans took refuge with the people on the west or Kwando side of the Zambezi, the rebels to the east or Kafue side.

[3] Malaria, which was then prevalent in the Zambezi Valley during the wet summer season.

November, 1885

I wonder the Dr. was so foolish as to come to the Zambesi, know-ing it as he does, at this unhealthy time of year. However, I hope Mrs. H. may escape; she is a very pleasant, lady-like person, and I pass many a pleasant hour away talking to her, the Dr. being very busy packing specimens and writing his journal, and another thing 'a woman's comforting and pleasant kind ways' has a sooth-ing and refining influence on we poor semi-barbarian interior hunters, traders and pioneers, for which we can never be too thankful. Don't smile when you read this, for it's a solemn fact, and although we do not always at once take heed, still their advice and good wishes sink deep.

Night of the 13th two men arrived from Shesheki, having been sent by the chiefs (who have taken refuge in the island) to me to go to Shesheki, and in a council which will be held, for me to try and settle their differences and reunite them, a boat having been sent for me to the junction of the Chobe and Zambesi; but as we are having rain day and night and am not quite able to go, nearly everyone at this place being down with fever, I am obliged to decline for the present. However, as soon as my wagon arrives will go to that place and from thence to the valley.

The Jesuits, who have been located here for the last five years are now very busy packing their goods to retire from here to a farm they have bought close to the Transvaal.[1] They have found that trying to civilise the native or heathen is a failure in these parts and have given it up. Coillard, however, the French mission-ary, is at Shesheki but has received orders from Leboche to remain at that place until I have been to the valley, as all his overtures have been made to the King who has fled, viz, Wa-ga-Funa,[2] and I must first make things agreeable for C. before he will be per-mitted to go on; which means simply that he won't see the Ba-rotse [Valley] before next winter. So much for being strong-

---

[1] Brother de Sadeleer abandoned the Pandamatenga station in December 1885.

[2] Coillard and his English artisan, Middleton, travelled from Seseheke to Lealui and return, December 1884 to February 1885. Coillard saw Akufuna and his Ngambela, Mataa, who offered the Frenchman a site for his proposed station at the village of Sefula.

G. Dorehill. Camel Hunting–22nd April 1875

The rider is George D. Dorehill, a hunter and trader who joined the party at Shoshong and travelled with it to Barotseland. He was the son of a British major-general and came to South Africa in 1871 to go to Kimberley. In the next year he went to Matabeleland, and until his death in the 1880's he lived and travelled in what are today Southern Rhodesia and the Bechuanaland Protectorate; he was at the Zambezi and in Barotseland during 1875–1876 and 1876–1877.

Giraffes, a good source of meat, were often called 'camels' from the Afrikaans name, *kameelperd*. This is acacia (thorn) and sand country between Shoshong and the southeastern end of the Makarikari.

Nos. 47 and 48

The Big Drummer and Dancers. Sesheke

The drummer is doubtless a member of the King's Nkoya band. He walks astride the long conical wooden drum, which is fastened to his waist.

Masked *makishi* dancers represent spirits intimately connected with the circumcision ceremonies of the Mbunda and other Mwiko tribes of North-Western Rhodesia. Many masked representations are found some of which have lost their original status and at an early time became adapted for professional entertainment. Sipopa seems to have had at least two such professional dancers at his court. One of the most popular is the dance of *Nalindele*, the young girl, who performs acrobatics on a rope stretched between two tall posts. The masks were often elaborate, made from painted barkcloth stretched over a withy framework or carved from wood, and were usually worn with a loosely knitted costume of wild sisal string which was worked in a pattern of broad bands and covered the whole body.

No. 33

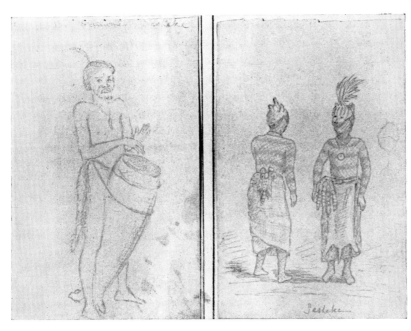

No. 47   No. 48

No. 49

No. 50

No. 49

Sepopa's Band. Sesheke

Sepopo had a private band of about twenty performers on drums, marimbas, native stringed instruments, iron bells, rattles, and pipes made of ivory, reeds, or wood. Only eight or ten musicians usually attended him, and they also shouted his praises as they serenaded him when he entered the town, attended festivities, or received strangers. The short, hourglass-shaped double drums and the marimbas were suspended from the neck by a strap. The marimbas consisted of strips of wood of varying length with calabash resonators beneath, and they were played with drumsticks. Drums were struck with the tips of the fingers or the palms of the hands.

No. 50

Travelling on the Zambesi

The three white men of the party being transported on the tree-lined river, one European and his baggage to each dugout canoe. Men of the riverine tribes were expert boatmen, and they poled the large canoes by working in rhythm. Passengers rode sitting down to avoid upsetting the delicate balance of these craft.

headed and refusing, or at all events, not taking my advice. Do not think I am egotistical, but it's a fact that people coming to the Zambesi will find all their efforts for whatever cause fruitless, if I refuse to help them. But it's not much to be wondered at when I tell you that I have lived amongst the natives here for fifteen years, and that those who were boys when I arrived are now men, and trust me. I have kept the Jesuits out to assist Coillard, who asked me in 1878, although he does not listen to my advice, and I suppose I must now help C. to get to the Barotse. It's a thankless office, for missionaries as far as I know them, with very few exceptions, generally when they have got all they can from one, throw you away like one throws away a fruit skin after having sucked out all the fruit. However, we shall see. C.'s niece was married at She-sheki on the 3rd [of] this month[1] to another missionary who came with them from Europe, a Mr. John Mairet. I was invited to the wedding, but considered a small journey of 60 miles on horseback, 12 on foot and 60 per boat to arrive there, and then return, making in all 264 miles, rather too much for any pleasure to be derived in witnessing the union of two loving hearts, so just sent my hearty congratulations but did not go.

Soon after, other messengers arrived, begging me to go and try and settle their differences; so on Tuesday I left Panda Matenka with four of my hunters, got to Leshoma on Wednesday; off again and in heavy rain arrived at Mamboowa (this Mamboowa is a large Mashubia town, belonging to an old friend of mine, Magumpa)[2] but had to wait all Friday getting boats and boatmen ready. However, next morning made an early start, shot two

[1] Jeanmairet, a Swiss, and Elise Coillard were married at Sesheke on 4 November 1885.

[2] Makumba, keeper of the southern gateway to Barotseland and headman of the village of Mambova. Makumba, a very intelligent Masubia, presided over the town of Impalera in 1875, was headman of Mambova in the 1880's, and in 1892 he built the new frontier village at Kazungula at the King's order. He died there during June 1895.

The Masubia were a tributary tribe living on the lower Chobe river and on both sides of the Zambezi up to Sesheke. They were boatmen, fishermen, and potters.

November, 1885

pukas[1] and one goose during the day, slept at Semalagha[2] and on
Sunday at 4 P.M. arrived at Shesheki, where I found the Rev. Coillard and party, all well but naturally nervous. The town deserted,
as all the headmen refuse to return to it before they hear that things
are satisfactorily settled in the Barotse Valley.

Received an ox from Maransian to kill, and another from the
chiefs who are fled to the island, so had plenty to eat. I remained
visiting amongst and reasoning with them till the following Saturday, but could effect nothing satisfactory; those on the island
being for the King and against Maransian, whom they would like
to kill, and Maransian knowing their kind intentions is prepared
for any emergency and has already sent a good troop of cattle
ahead to some of his dependants living at Victoria Falls. If affairs
get too hot for him he will cross through to Panda Matenga and
seek protection from me. Those are his present intentions. It is
impossible to see how things will end, but they could scarcely be
worse than they are at present. Everyone goes about fully armed
and none of the opposing chiefs will meet.

Seeing that I could effect nothing, I left Shesheki, arriving
again at Leshoma on the 30th, and made ready to start for Panda
Matenga on Tuesday. But late on Monday night, after I had retired to rest, a man arrived from Shesheki asking for Joros (me)[3]
and begging me to return again and try to put affairs right again
between them. So on Wednesday, I started again with Blockley[4]
and others of my hunters (our party now numbering ten breech
loaders), whom I started on foot from Mamboowa on Thursday,

[1] The puku, a water antelope. See frontispiece.
[2] Simalaha Flats between Machili and Zambezi rivers.
[3] Holub recorded that Westbeech was called *Joros Mtunya, Big George*, by the
Africans to distinguish him from George Blockley, who was known as *Little George*
to them.
[4] George Blockley, who went to the Zambezi with Westbeech in 1871 and became the latter's best-known agent in that region. He hunted and traded for Westbeech and managed his storehouses at Pandamatenga, the Chobe mouth, and Sesheke.
Blockley was a genial man who knew the Barotse and their country well, and he gave
all European travellers a hospitable welcome and a helping hand. Except for occasional journeys to the Transvaal, he lived in Zambezia till his death in August 1887.

December, 1885–January, 1886

intending to follow per boat at once, but was detained all that day and Friday by heavy rains, but arrived again at Shesheki on Sunday where again I received an ox to kill and on Monday saw all the chiefs at a big palaver which I held, and everyone was armed and in their war paint. I reasoned long with them and told all to return to their town of Shesheki, that those who did so would show that they were Leboche's people and those who would not return would show that they were not.

Also after listening patiently to their oratory of what they had done and could and would do, I just simply told them that any outbreak now would be taken by me as a sign that they did not acknowledge Leboche, and with those who were loyal and my hunters armed with breech loaders, we could just try the issue, and they knew that every gun pointed by me and my hunters meant one or more of the rebels shot for each bullet. This had the desired effect and the next day they commenced bringing their cattle in and making their town habitable.

I then left for Panda Matenga, to make ready for my trip to see the King in the valley and on the 29th December again left Panda Matenga and after sundry delays I at last on Saturday, 9th January 1886 crossed at the junction of Chobe and Zambesi, having had three boats sent me by Magumpa, on arriving at whose town found beer plentiful, but rain more so. He would not hear of my pitching my tent anywhere but in the middle of his enclosure, which I did, and here I am 'au present' awaiting events.

10*th*, 11*th*, 12*th*. Rain any amount but as our meat was not, went out, and thanks to two breech loaders shot two rooi bucks,[1] one goose and three ducks. Next day two rooi bucks again, but as I am in the middle of the town and many hungry stomachs knocking about, a lot of meat goes but a very little way together today. My own crew consists entirely of his own men. Am now only awaiting Ratouw's[2] boat, which might have been here days ago, as

[1] The rooibok or impala (*Aepyceros melampus*), an antelope of medium size.

[2] The titles of some of the other headmen of Sesheke were: Ratau (Father of Lions), Mokhole, Katukula, Nalishuwa, Tahalima. This Ratau was very influential and a supporter of Lewanika.

January, 1886

it is only four miles away. However, he says it will come tomorrow, but on the morrow we saw nothing of it. He says he will send at once for it, and I am most anxious for its arrival as the rapids[1] will be getting more dangerous and I have eighteen men to feed and nothing for them to eat. Magumpa left for his town early this morning in a very heavy rain, but he is so tired of this place and its hunger that he is not to be deterred by the rain.

Monday 25*th.* Down came the rain again, but as I had packed the boats early and was thoroughly sick of this place, I started. The headmen made me a present of a young ox as meat for the road. I had it driven on to Soka's town, about four miles from Shesheki, where I meant to kill it, but it broke away from the boys and took to the river, which I suppose I was meant to cross. It had not gone far before a crocodile convinced it of the futility of such an attempt and went away with my beef. The boys returned to Shesheki and reported the fact to the headmen, who kindly sent me another. It I killed, although it was raining hard and slept at Soka's. Heard that Shesheki natives had stolen and killed a beast (ox or cow?) belonging to the Revd. C. but whether he knows about it, can't say and have no chance of letting him know.

Tuesday. Still raining and the wind very strong; however, I packed everything snugly and started. In crossing the river at Island of the Matabele[2] two of my three boats were nearly capsized; the one in which sat a hunter of mine, by a hippopotamus, and mine by the wind. However, we managed at 2 P.M. to get to Somalumba's village[3] and commenced making as snug sleeping places as possible with wet grass on wetter ground, and the day closed in still raining. It is most miserable. Wood scarce, everything damp and all hands growly (a good word, that).

---

[1] The rapids in the Zambezi between Sesheke and Lealui. The rains were filling the rivers.

[2] The island on which a Matabele impi, sent by Mzilikazi to attack the Makololo and the Barotse, was marooned by its pressed boatmen. This occurred during the 1840's. The Matabele soldiers were there subdued by hunger and were then killed or captured by their enemies.

[3] Perhaps Simalumba, in 1875 a Masubia chief.

Forgot to note that when the Barotse killed Maransian's uncle in Shesheki they cut his body into small pieces, so that the vultures would have more ease in eating it.[1] With him were also assegaied eight of his people.

Made an early start but the wind was so strong that we had to lay to, arriving late at Katongo.[2] This is the place where Sepopa (their greatest chief) was driven from in 1876 by his people. Here I shall remain over and mend the boats, which are leaking as only native dug outs know how to ; and to make ropes to assist us in hauling the boats through the rapids.

Early away again and on Friday arrived at the N'gambwe Cataracts.[3] In all my journeys to the valley have never seen so many hippos and so much elephant spoor as I have during the last two days. I also met natives from the King, who report things and His Majesty quietly settled, and that H.M. is most anxious for my arrival. As the boats had thus far had a rough time of it coming through the rapids, I was detained all Saturday having them re-sewn, but made another start on Sunday for the Injoko River.[4] Here I stay over one day to shoot game and dry it for the onward journey, as game is plentiful here, though it's rather dangerous at this time of the year buffalo shooting, as the cows are now calving and will charge at once. This in thorn thickets very dense and grass at least seven feet high is rather serious work, and one is on them before you know it. I shot a fat cow and returned to camp with frightful headache, which seems inclined to be frequent with me this trip, for I have them every mid-day. Got the boys to cup me with a native cupping horn ;[5] sent out three boys to try their luck ; had blankets etc. put in the sun to get the mildew smell out

[1] The attack of December 1885. See note 3, page 33.

[2] Katonga Village, headman Sikhosi, two days' journey above Sesheke and the last Masubia town.

[3] Ngambwe Rapids, made by a natural barrier of rock in the river. Canoes could be hauled up them if lightened of their loads. This was a portage of 800 yards.

[4] The Njoko or Snake River, a tributary of the Zambezi coming from the northeast. Its mouth is at about 17° 7' south latitude.

[5] The Africans used a horn for cupping or bleeding. The large end was placed over the wound and a partial vacuum formed by sucking on the small end.

January–Febuary, 1886

of them, and boys returned late having also shot a buffalo cow. So ends January and during the whole month have had only two fine days, but even the nights of them were wet.

Wednesday, 3rd February. Arrived at Matomi's,[1] where I met some people sent by Moremi (Chief of Lake N'gami)[2] to me, even if they had to go to Panda Matenga with kind messages and a request for me to visit him, also if there was any hunting veldt belonging to him that I should like to shoot in. Also kind messages and intimations about which he would like to talk to me personally, but of which he only sent me a hint. I sent him word that if he sent people to escort me next September I should be very happy to visit him.

Arrived at Seoma[3] on the 5th, guided by Matomi, who went ahead in a small sea cow boat[4] to pilot us through the rapids, which when the river is full as it is now are very dangerous about Seoma. Found the villages deserted by all but a few women, so sent out my boatmen to see if they can collect any people to carry the boats round the Gonye Falls,[5] a distance of four miles and shall have to stay here till they do. Still have the headaches and today, Saturday, is a particularly head-achy and enlarged spleen day, so much so that I can neither enjoy food or pipe.

Sunday. Got a few people but not nearly enough, but as the chief of the town has also arrived and sent on the same errand, expect to get the boats transported tomorrow. Any amount of headache, so had my head rubbed with camphor liniment which has helped a little, but very little. Short of meat for my boatmen, so two of my boys who can shoot will try their luck tomorrow.

---

[1] Matome's small village, near Matome Island and above the confluence of the Zambezi and the Lumbe rivers.

[2] Moremi II (died 1890), chief of the Tawana, a Bechuana tribe living at Lake Ngami. He succeeded his father, Lechulatebe, on the latter's death in August 1874.

[3] Sioma, a village about one mile *above* the Gonye Falls during the 1880's. Westbeech seems confused here.

[4] A canoe for use in hunting hippos.

[5] Gonye Falls, which boats and loads were portaged round. On the south bank there is a perpendicular drop of water about thirty feet high and ninety to a hundred yards wide.

Tried it but returned without anything. So next morning we started and on the way I shot a koodoo and two rooi bucks (pallahs) and on the following Tuesday we arrived at Nalolo,[1] but my headaches were so bad that I was unable to see the Queen,[2] so she sent me an ox to kill and came herself twice a day to see me. I was there three days but left on Saturday for the King's where I arrived on Sunday but very sick. The King keeps sending to the graves of the old departed Barotse Kings to pray for my recovery. But the 'Dear Departed' have been very deaf to all the prayers for my recovery, for the headache is nearly unbearable and my spleen very sore and very much swollen. Refugees arrive every day and those who are of any importance and have fought against Luwanika are led away to execution and common ones given as slaves to the newly appointed chiefs or the crocodiles. As there is nothing worth writing about here, I will just give you a short account of the rebellion.

There has been since Sepopa's days a family of great importance amongst the Barotse called the Banosha and who were the prime movers in the insurrections against Sepopa and N'gwanawena and now again against Luwanika, whom they succeeded in driving away in September 1884. Early one morning they collected at the King's town of Li-a-Liue[3] and fired several shots into his hut but without killing him. He seized a breech loader, fired at them and succeeded in killing one man, and in the confusion of women's

---

[1] Nalolo, the town of the Mulena Mukwae on the right bank of the Zambezi. It was three-quarters of a mile from the river, on a large mound, and in 1895 it had a population of 1500 to 2000.

[2] The Mulena Mukwae, then Lewanika's twin sister and the next most important person in the tribe. By Barotse custom, the King's sisters and other female blood relatives were given special rank and a share in the government. They were treated like men, were addressed by male titles, and were permitted to choose their own husbands (one at a time) and change them at will. Several Mukwaes were local chiefs. The senior or Mulena Mukwae, of Nalolo, governed a province and was consulted by the King in all important matters of state; she was a fierce partisan of her brother's, and, though reputedly a matrimonial spider, was also said to have been humane enough to deplore the bloodshed in her country. She died in 1934.

[3] Lealui. Established as capital by Sipopa, re-established as such by Lewanika when he became King. He was building his quarters there in August 1878. The town was near the Zambezi, in a swampy, very fertile valley that was inundated every year.

February, 1886

cries and burning huts, fled out with the loaded gun but the wrong belt of cartridges. Three of his people and his oldest but still young son, Leteah,[1] fled with him.

Outside the town he halted to see what was going on, but as he had been seen and they were shooting at him, he again let drive amongst the crowd and killed another, and going to reload, then found that he had the wrong cartridge belt, so had to bolt. The rebels, seeing that two of their number had fallen and thinking he was well armed, let him proceed without further opposition, so he went towards the Linyanti River, being joined in the afternoon by his old Prime Minister, Selumbu, who has also after assegaing one, managed to escape, and they after a few days managed to get to the Mashi country.[2] There after some time he was joined by some loyals and proceeded with them west to Lebebe's country,[3] the chief of which place received them well and found food and cattle for him and his people.

From here he sent Selumbu to Moremi, chief of Lake N'gami to ask for assistance, who at once sent him some cattle and a wagon-load of corn and promised that as soon as the war in which he was engaged with the Matabele[4] was finished, that he would go at once to his assistance. By this time Mataha, Chief of the Ba-no-Sha, had sent for another member of Sepopa's family named Tatela (a nephew who came at once and was appointed King). But many were against him and collecting under Samaseku, brother-

[1] Litia, then fourteen years old. He became a Christian, was living at Kazungula in 1895, and succeeded his father in 1916 under the title of Yeta III.

[2] The country of the tribes about the lower Kwando or Mashi River, to the west of Barotseland. The tribal groups there are the Mampukushu, Makangale, Makangwale, Makoba or Yei, and Mashi.

[3] Libebe (a dynastic name), chief of the Mampukushu at Andara Island in the Okavango River. His people, good watermen and related to the Ovambo of South West Africa, migrated from the swamps of the Chobe. He was a renowned rainmaker.

[4] The Matabele attacked the Tawana at their home round Lake Ngami in 1883, and they were partly successful in that they captured many cattle. The surprised Bechuanas took refuge in the swamps. When the Matabele came again in 1885, the Tawana, well-armed with breechloaders, were ready for them and killed a great many of the raiders.

in-law of Lewanika, and thinking if they won to get back their old King, they fought a battle about 12 miles from Li-a-Liue and were worsted. Samaseku and some hundreds were killed (37 took refuge in some garden huts, were found there, secured inside, the huts set on fire and they were roasted inside). Those who survived the fight fled to Lewanika, who was still at Lebebe's and daily increasing his forces.

Now began Mataha to show his nature. Having all the power in his own hands, Tatela being only king in name, he began killing off all who were still loyal, or whom he thought were. Lewanika's mother, brothers and any of his family or children he could get hold of, were butchered. And so he kept murdering until the month of August 1885, when the King (Lewanika) sent a good force under Selumbu to enter the valley from the south and so proceed towards Li-a-Liue, collecting as he went. This he did, but found when he arrived close to that town that Mataha, Tatela, and all who were of their party had fled to Sekofella (brother of Tatela),[1] King of a tract of country about five days' journey from the Barotse border. So Selumbu remained master of the valley, augmenting his forces, and sent word to Lewanika to return. Mataha had in the meantime deposed Tatela from the kingship and appointed his brother Sekofella to that dignity, who accepted, and collecting all his forces and as many of the surrounding tribes (clans) as would follow him, started for the valley to take possession of his new country.

In the meantime, Lewanika had advanced, and hearing that Mataha was close by, divided his army into four divisions and awaited his approach outside of Li-a-Liue, but close to that town and so placed them that only Selumbu's force could be seen by Mataha, who came on confidently in one immense column. Selumbu boldly met him, and after some close fighting and skirmishing which gave time to Lewanika gradually to surround Mataha, but

[1] Mataa, the rebel Ngambela, made Sikufele, another descendent of Mulambwa and ancestor of the present chief in the Kabompo district, king and became his Ngambela.

46

February, 1886

when Selumbu fell the fight began in earnest and lasted from about 10 A.M. to 3 P.M. when Mataha, Sekofella, and all the head-men and hundreds on both sides being down (for it was close assegai fighting, very few guns being used) Mataha's army, find-ing themselves nearly without leaders, threw down their shields and fled.

Now began the rout and slaughter, and the flat from Li-a-Liue to Mongu (Imongi),[1] a distance of 12 miles without a bush, is even now covered with skeletons and grinning skulls, as there was no hiding place, it being the month of November and the grass only an inch or two high. Selumbu was the only one that received funeral honours. The King now, I am sorry to say, began to show his capacity in the killing line, for all who were caught or came to surrender themselves, trusting to his former clemency, were im-mediately killed; even the women, wives of rebels, were ripped open by the assegai and thus left to die. Others were taken to the plain to what is called the Wizard's Ant-heap,[2] their arms and legs broken and left for the wolves to finish or die of hunger, thirst and pain. Boys and girls of any tender age were carried off to the nearest lagoons and thrown to the crocodiles, which swarm in them, and by all I can gather, as many, if not more, were killed by these means, than fell in the fight.

Moremi, Chief of Lake N'gami came through the Zambesi according to promise with about forty horsemen and a lot of foot-men, to Lewanika's assistance but found the fighting over and the country settling down again; so staying but a short time and receiving many of the rebels and as many of the old Makololo tribe as wished to go with him, and a large troop of cattle as presents, he started for his own country. Such had been the state of things in this delightful country, of which when I am in the valley, I belong to the Council; and though the missionaries are

---

[1] Mongu, a promontory sticking out into the flood-plain. Selected by Livingstone as a suitable site for a mission station and now the present Government Headquarters in the Barotseland Protectorate.

[2] The mound close to Lealui on which the Paris Mission Society built its mission station of Luatile and so called because witches were burnt on it.

coming for I have got the Jesuits ousted and Coillard in, I think [it] will take many years to civilise its King and people, leave alone Christianizing them. So much for the war and its ending, though one good thing seems to have happened by it, which is that the King has become more manly and appears to have a much more stable character.

March 5th. Last night a theft was committed in the house of one of the princesses whilst asleep. It appears the thief entered, asked her where her two lechwe karosses[1] were and her setutinga kaross. She, thinking she was speaking to one of her slaves, told him to look on the line at the other end of the hut and not bother and to be careful to close the door well, that thieves, wizards, and mosquitoes could not enter, which he did and decamped with the karosses. Scotland Yard has not succeeded in recovering the property yet, though they know the thief and are on the trail.

Wonderful to relate, I have been without any ailment for five days, from the 9th to today, the 15th; I suppose to make up for it, have been doctored and plastered by the King's M.D.'s to their hearts content and my intense disgust, but to please the King who is really anxious, I grin and bear it. No one has been allowed to enter my compound (skerum)[2] during my last sharp attack except my own servants, so have had the benefit of being quiet and could thus use my own medicines sub-rosa, although accepting but quietly burying their nostrums, but the plasterings, scrapings, and scarrifyings I had to endure. I shall now, in a few days ask for the road,[3] as I have done all I came about and am anxious to return. King started on a round of visits to the graves of his forefathers to pray for the welfare of his country, but being too weak could not accompany him. He was away four days, returning on the 5th with much beating of drums and acclamations of the crowds.

[1] Robes of fur or prepared hide that served as cloaks and blankets. See sketch 31.

[2] A skerm, a semicircular fence of branches or thorn bushes built against the wind. This was usually a temporary shelter, but the living place so named here must have been a more elaborate and comfortable dwelling.

[3] To ask a native ruler for his permission to travel a road under his control. A Sindebele idiom.

March, 1886

18*th*. Received letters from Panda Matenka. All well there. Also one from Dr. Holub asking me to get permission for him to cross the Zambesi at its junction with the Chobe, so that he could have an easier route to the Mashukulumbwe[1] country. This I did and gained the King's permission, only was not able to get people from the King to go the entire journey with him, owing to the still unsettled state of the country and so many of his people still being refugees. Had it not have been so, would have assisted him to the utmost. Also today settle the last of my affairs and have got the Linyanti country as hunting grounds. Had a long talk with Felisberto Guedes Sousa,[2] a Portuguese trader from Benguella on the west coast, about Major Serpa Pinto.[3] He laughs as does everyone else about here, about the night attack by the Barotse and the gallant little Major's fight with them (for at this very town of Li-a-Liue the supposed fight took place which was lit up only by burning huts) also his great explorings, and simply says, as I have always maintained, that he just came with the trading footpath from the west coast, and then continued his route with boats and people lent him by Lewanika and they took him to the Englishman's wagon road at Leshuma, where he was picked up by the Rev. Coillard and taken south. His concluding remark was graphic. He has written a deal but done nothing worthy, excepting in Khame's country,[4] where he shot two lions in the night by lamp light with the right and left barrels of his gun 'Good Shot.' Great man! You should get his book and see the pictures of fight and shooting the lions.

Have succeeded in saving the Rev. Coillard a great expense by getting the King to make the wagon road from Shesheki through Luangha Valley (which is nearly all thick forest and infested with

[1] Mashukulumbwe was the name given by the Barotse to the Ba-Ila of the middle Kafue Valley and upper waters of the Zambezi tributaries on the south. The Barotse exercised a loose sort of sovereignty over them. See sketches 54 and 55.

[2] Not otherwise identified.

[3] A Portuguese army officer and would-be explorer. His book is listed in the Bibliography. Westbeech's estimate of him is correct.

[4] Khama, chief of the Mangwato at Shoshong.

the dreaded tsetse fly)[1] by turning four Matotella towns to the work, instead of leaving it to the missionaries as was at first intended.

King sent messengers to his sister, Queen of Nalolo, advising her of my arrival and for her to prepare food for me. The King's eldest son Leteah and nephew have asked his permission to accompany me on a visit to Panda Matenka. This he has granted and made them over to me to look after. His son is about fourteen, and nephew Le Koguani (the Beetle) about sixteen. It shows they must have great faith in me, as a Kafir never likes parting with his children especially sons, and Leteah is the heir apparent to the Barotse throne. So began making ready for the return trip and should have started today the 23rd but as we heard the Rev. C. was close by, the King asked me to stay a few days until he became acquainted with him.[2] Did so, and got finally away on the 29th.

Stayed with Mugui (the Queen) the 30th, who slaughtered an ox for us, and came on steadily, collecting food at all the towns, for our party numbered fifty-five in seven boats, and on the 7th April arrived at Injoko, my old camping ground on every trip to get a supply of meat, and here I shot three buffaloes, two rooi bucks and [a] puku ram. Dried the meat and on the 8th arrived at N'gambwe Cataract, where I saw a lot of people camped and drying elephant meat. Went to talk with them and on my asking for news, for that is always the first question after greeting in the interior, received a large packet of letters, and was I not glad, for I had long been longing for news from home and now I had it, besides letters from friends from different parts of the world, but first and most longed for the ones from home, for every poor wandering Englishman, no matter where settled, always looks upon and calls England home. Was it not a strange post office at which I received them? I think it enhanced their interest. Fancy, in a wild part of the interior, at the N'gambwe Cataracts on the Zambesi, the cataracts in front of me roaring and flashing their

[1] The Luanja, a tributary from the north that enters the Zambezi near Sesheke.
[2] Coillard saw Lewanika and Westbeech at Lealui during March-April 1886.

April, 1886

spray in the sun, Kafirs all round me greeting my boatmen and asking about the rapids through which we had safely passed, but which they had still to risk, for they were with boats (and the river is now dangerous, being at its fullest), as I smiled at anything that amused me in the letters and quietly remarking to one another, 'Look, he's laughing again. How wonderful! What can he see in that thing that he's looking at that causes such pleasure? For he does not speak, neither does it. Surely there's only one thing that beats white men and that's death. See how they cure sickness and that without even asking for payment.' That and a lot of other talk was going on, but I had the reading of many (though occasionally I would sneak one out of my pocket and have a look), as the sun was getting low and the boats had to be carried and dragged round the cataracts so as to make an early start on the morrow.

At daybreak parted from the natives who had brought my letters, as they were proceeding to the King (but not without making them wish for another 'post chance') and arrived that evening at Katongo. I intend to cross the river here when I have collected my hunters and look up the Linyanti elephants.

The next day saw us at Shesheki, where I visited the mission party, who were well, but anxious about Mr. C. who was still at the King's. However, as I had left him in good health and could assure them that they might expect him any day as he was to have left Li-a-Liue shortly after me, that comforted them. I remained four days at Shesheki, the headmen of that place all wishing to show their respect for the young Prince who was with me, by giving him as much food as they could, so during the four days we were there he killed six oxen, and I two which were easily disposed of by our party.

We then on the fifth morning left, arriving the same afternoon at Mamboowa, where I met Blockley, who had come to meet me. Here I stayed one day to allow Leteah and party time for drinking some sixty gallons of beer which had been made for them, and left for Leshuma, where after being two days, the wagons for which I had sent to Panda Matenka for from Shesheki arrived.

No. 51

Linyanti or Tchobe. 14th June

A small native canoe on the Linyanti or Chobe River, a tributary
of the Zambezi that joins it about fifty miles above the Victoria
Falls. The road from the south to the Zambezi country ended at
their junction, where the large 'island' of Impalera is located. The
Chobe rises in southeastern Angola and is called the Kwando
above the large swamps that it forms during the rains in the
Bechuanaland Protectorate.

No. 52

Sea Cow on the River Chobe

The hippopotamus was very numerous in the Zambezi and its
tributaries. It was often called the 'sea cow,' a translation of the
Afrikaans name, *seekoei*. The palm trees are the ilala, doum, or
vegetable ivory species (*Hyphoene ventricosa*), which grows very
tall on the banks and islands of these rivers.

No. 51

No. 52

№. 53

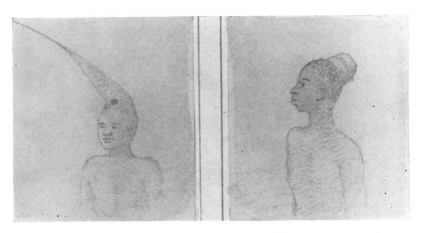

№. 54   №. 55

No. 53

Sepopa–King of the Barotse Nation

In 1875 Sipopa was about thirty-five years old and wore European clothes and an ostrich feather in his hat, as Fairlie here pictures him. He was the son of Mulambwa, the Barotse chief before
that tribe was conquered by the Makololo, an invading horde
from Bechuanaland. When the Barotse overthrew the Makololo
about 1864 or 1865, Sipopa became the ruler of the Barotse.
Because of his cruelty to his subjects, and his setting aside of
traditional law and custom, he was killed by rebellious subjects in
1876. This portrait, embellished by the engraver, appears at page
220 of Volume II of Holub's *Seven Years in South Africa*. Holub
met Fairlie in Barotseland, and undoubtedly the artist gave the
Czech traveller a copy.

Nos. 54 and 55

Headdresses of a tribe North of the Zambesi

These men are Mashukulumbwe or Baila, a tribe of the middle
Kafue River valley. Six of them were at Sipopa's with token presents when Fairlie and his companions and Dr. Holub were there.
The *isusu* headdress on the left was based on a shaving from a
sable antelope horn, round which the individual's own hair was
drawn up and plaited into a fine net. The hair of relatives was also
added, and sometimes this unusual coiffure was four to five feet
high. Its purpose was said to have been to help warriors and
hunters keep in touch with each other in the tall grass of the Kafue
Flats.

May–June, 1886

Here I had a two days' relapse of fever, but taking one wagon for self and traps and one for Leteah and his cousin, their retinue, however, walking and carrying calabashes of water, after two days and nights wagoning arrived at Panda Matenka all well. For myself I can only say that for many years I have not been so unwell as I was from the commencement of the year until the month of May. Accordingly, on the 31st May I left Panda Matenka again, accompanied by Watson (my partner)[1] and my hunters, Watson to remain at Gazungula (where I am going to build a new store at the junction of the Zambesi and Chobe rivers)[2] and I to proceed to my new hunting grounds of Linyanti.

However, on my arrival at Leshuma on the 2nd June, I received a letter from the Rev. C. saying that the Barotse were at Shesheki, having been sent by the King to trade with me. So I came on to Gazungula and Watson started back for Panda Matenka with the wagons to get the goods for me to trade with. I also sent off my hunters to wait for me at the Inquesi River,[3] where game is plentiful and where I can easily rejoin them after I have traded with the Barotse.

Found Dr. Holub still here as he could get no carriers, the headmen about here casting every obstacle in his way. I did what I could for him, saying that the King would be very dissatisfied with them if he heard about it, for having given the road to the Dr. to travel through his country, it would be expected he would have no further trouble. This having been granted by the King at my intercession, I should certainly report matters to him. This, and

[1] Frank Watson, a trader. In the winter of 1884 he brought two wagon loads of goods to Westbeech at the Zambezi. Like Harry Ware, he conducted English sportsmen to the Falls and the Barotse country.

[2] This spot was named for a large German sausage tree (*Kigelia pinnata*), called *mzungula* in Sikalanga. A mission station was founded on the north bank of the Zambezi at the Chobe mouth in 1889 by M. and Mme. Louis Jalla of Coillard's group, and in 1892 Lewanika ordered a village built at the station. This place became known as Kazungula. Westbeech's new store was probably opposite the old site of Impalera Village.

[3] The Ngwezi River, a tributary of the Zambezi draining from the east above the Victoria Falls. Its mouth is between Kazungula and Sesheke.

June, 1886

Leteah also siding with me, to whom I had sent a private message, had the desired effect and got the long looked for carriers and two responsible headmen were also given him for the first stage of his journey, others were then to relieve them from place to place to the confines of the Bashukulumbwe country. I think, however, that it will go hard with the Dr. as this nation cannot be depended on and the Bashukulumbwe are a wild treacherous lot. I do not for a moment think that he will succeed in carrying out his present intentions of reaching the Congo, but expect to see him turn up again at Panda Matenka or to hear of his having gone to the Portuguese settlements on the east coast.

Well, on the 10th June we got the Dr. started, two of his Austrian servants having started a few days previously with a batch of carriers whom the Dr. had engaged. One of his servants died at Panda Matenka and one at Leshuma. He has had many losses, and now I wish him and his plucky wife every success, though I wish it had been Englishmen instead of Austrians exploring the interior from this side.

It is now winter, but the mosquitoes don't seem to think so, for do their best to keep us lively and warm at night. Watson arrived on the night of the 15th June with the goods, so I traded the Barotse ivory, a fine lot of bull, got my few things ready and on Saturday 19th started for the Linyanti hunting grounds. Got a boat from Mamboowa, but as it had to be repaired, did not get away from that town before the 22nd. Heard there were plenty of elephants in the Linyanti so expect to do well.

A great beer-drinking yesterday as a farewell to Leteah. Natives all fearfully drunk but they seemed to enjoy it. I was thankful when the sun set for then we had a little quiet, but at about 9 P.M. the drums were set to work, and with drumming, dancing and screaming, for you can't call it singing, the day broke. I slept pretty well through it all, for I'm well used to noise, and before the sun rose I was loading my boat and Leteah's party had to follow suit, although I expect they felt the effects of last night's and yesterday's debauch.

June, 1886

Whilst rowing, picked up a lechi ram that had just been drowned by a crocodile whilst swimming through the river. It was still warm and the meat accordingly good. Got to Semalagha where we slept, and making an early start thence, got to Shesheki at sunset. Here I found my hunters already arrived, and as they had expected me, my sleeping place [was] already made and about two feet thickness of nice, soft, sweet, fresh grass laid down to form my mattress.

Visited the Rev. C. next day, who begged my acceptance of a silver watch as a recognition of his thanks for my endeavours in furthering his mission amongst the Barotse, which is now a settled thing. I accepted it with suitable words, which pleased him, and I was pleased, not on account of the watch, but simply because he evidently appeared grateful for my services. I have done much for my countrymen in this and other countries (Kafir) but it is the only time I have received a little gratitude. In future, I shall let people pay for my experience, as it was not gained without considerable expense.

The chiefs of Shesheki have all gone to the valley to welcome back the King and to return with the new Maransian,[1] who is the King's nephew, so perhaps things will now go smoothly. However, I was not without food, as I received a present of a slaughter cow from an old friend, which I killed and divided the meat amongst my people and started them on for Katongo, where I cross the Zambesi for Linyanti. Shall leave here per boat and rejoin them on Sunday. This I did after twelve hours good rowing and found them at the village at Katongo, but as they had shot nothing along the road, neither had I per river, we went to bed perfectly hungry, the beef being done. However, raised a pot of beer out of the old man of the town, Sokasi, and that had to suffice.

Commenced crossing hunters and carriers (86 all told) next morning; got to water at 2 P.M., left boys to make camp and

---

[1] Kabuku, eighteen or twenty years old and a son of the Mulena Mukwae, was installed as Mulasiane of Sesheke in August 1886.

June, 1886

started on foot again, though tired, to look for game, for with the exception of my coffee, honey (for sugar), tea and some meal for [an] occasional loaf, we had literally nothing for all hands this night to eat. We were not long before we came across fresh buffalo spoor which we followed about seven miles, caught up to them, becrept them and succeeded in killing four and wounding one so badly that the next morning I sent a boy to look it up. This he did and found it dead.

This fifth one I gave the people of the village living close to where we had camped. It was nearly 9 P.M. when we got back to camp, and I went to bed again supperless, excepting a strong cup of coffee, and I had had nothing since Sekosi's pot of beer yesterday. I was really done up, but the boys were not, for they danced, eat, cooked, eat again and slept, leaving one awake to mind the cooking and as soon as everything was ready for gorging, for eating you could not call it, at it they went again. The cook had the advantage, for whilst they slept he was roasting nice fat pieces and playing a lone hand, to his infinite satisfaction, and still at the general feed joining in with the crowd. I really don't know where they put it. As I could not sleep being too tired, I lay watching them, and it came into my head to give you a description of a native banquet. It seems the more sand it has about it, the more enjoyable it is, and sharpens either their teeth or appetites, perhaps both.

One of my Bushmen shot an eland cow (fat) but too far to return to camp in the night; so he cut up the animal in the night and came next morning bringing my meat. (For we have certain parts which they take care to keep clean.) For carriers it was very fat, so I rendered out the fat for future use with poor game and gave all the meat, except my own, to the boys.

Everyone is looking and feeling happy today, plenty of food and shining faces, though they do from fat. However, they are all pleased and so am I. I stayed over the next day to dry the meat, so that it will be lighter to carry. In the afternoon one of our gun carriers, not content with what he had and without orders, started off with three others to see what he could do. Wounded an old bull buffalo which got into long sedge grass on the edge of a swamp. The boy followed it in, shot at it, missed it, and at him it came (there was no chance of escape for him), breaking some ribs and laying a piece of his lung open to view and protruding through the ribs. His thigh was fearfully ripped open. He remained where he had been knocked down and the buffalo returned to his old retreat. One of the others returned with the news to camp and I sent bearers to carry him in. The gun, however, which he had thrown down when the buffalo charged him, remained there, no one daring to look for it. They brought him to camp late in the afternoon. I had everything ready and washed his wounds and bandaged them up, though I could see there was no hope. The wound was a fearful sight with the lung protruding ; it was a wonder his living even though carried to camp. He received his wound at about 3 P.M. and died at 2 A.M. next morning. We dug his grave and buried him before sunrise ; his townsmen, after we had filled it up, placed his assegais, knobkerrie, musical instrument (native piano) etc. over the grave and then sprinkled water over all.

We then went after the buffalo but he had got into such thick grass and reeds that it was too dangerous to follow him up, as one had to force your own way in by opening the grass and reeds in front, so we left it to the tender mercies of the lions. Its front leg was broken as we could see as we followed the spoor. We then went to the scene of yesterday's mishap, and after a deal of searching found the gun completely tramped into the mud, but not damaged so far and washing will make that all serene.

Returned to camp, fired a fusilade over the grave, and as it was still early, left for Impatcha,[1] a large pool which never dries, and after ten hours good walking we arrived at it on Thursday 1st July. Here we found any amount of elephant spoor, but old ; it is, however, the main drinking place and here I intend forming camp and sending out [hunters] N. S. E. W.

[1] Impatcha or Mpacha, a large pan about fifteen miles southwest of the Katima Mulilo Rapids in the Zambezi. It is reported to occasionally dry up at the present time.

THE DIARY OF GEORGE WESTBEECH

July, 1886

Yesterday we crossed the spoor of nine elephant bulls and to-morrow two of my people go after them and I stay and busy myself in making the camp comfortable and lion-proof, as here I have to stay with a few natives in charge of everything. Well, camp was formed, but the elephants after which the boys went, had crossed the Zambesi.

On the 2nd July I started John Weyers with nine boys; Africa and Hy. Wall[1] with seventeen; Skraal with seven and Adonis with seven. Jantje still being behind, [I] having sent him to Gazungula with orders for a 6-bore muzzle loading elephant gun and a 12-bore breech loader, he will come on our spoor (there being no paths in the forest) and on his arrival shall start him off also with seven boys. Old Klaas, young Klaas and Gert, I sent through from Shesheki. April, August and Andries are still in the Magelic,[2] April by report having shot a very large bull elephant (report turned out true). Expect them to turn up some day.

Sent out some boys to look for game, but they returned at sunset unlucky, got it but did nothing. As the pool of Impatcha is in an immense plain, I started this morning and had bush carried to five different spots to make shooting covers, so that we can remain unseen by any game coming to drink. It is also a protection from the sun whilst waiting for them. The amount of game that drinks here in the spring when the outlying waters dry up, must by the old spoor be enormous, for all round the vlei are footpaths of elephants, buffaloes, giraffe, eland, gnu, quagga,[3] etc. etc, so I expect to have some good shooting later on and shall have to make shoot-

---

[1] Jan Weyers, an Afrikaner who was employed by Westbeech as an elephant hunter during the 1880's; he was in the interior during the preceding decade. The Jan Afrikas, father and son, and Henry (Harry) Wall, were half-caste hunters who first appear on the interior scene in the 1870's. Wall and the younger Afrika outlived their employer by many years. Westbeech employed a good many elephant hunters, of all colours and tribes, and they were a very tough lot. It was a hard and dangerous life.

[2] The high grassy plain of the Machili River, which comes from the northeast and enters the Kasaya channel on the right bank about thirteen miles above the junction of the latter with the main Zambezi. The plain is about fifty miles long and is bounded on the south and west by the Zambezi, on the north and east by a forest. It was a paradise of game, and was Westbeech's permanent hunting veld, given him by Sipopa.

[3] Burchell's zebra.

ing pits. Boys went out again, returned unlucky, having only seen some gnu and two elands, at which they fired but without success as the grass was too thick and long to render shooting at running game certain, and unless natives (generally) can creep close up to game, their chances of returning with meat are very uncertain. There are exceptions but very few.

August arrived this afternoon, having shot an elephant cow in the Inguesi bush, then followed us on here. Shall have to go out myself and look for game and sleep out, as it is mostly too far to kill and return. Accordingly on Monday I started August off with thirteen boys on his hunt to N.W. and started off myself with some boys to look for game, as our pots and boys will soon be without the wherewithal to fill them, and that won't do. Engaged also five Manquoias[1] to go with hunters or carry ivory, in fact for any work.

The Manquoia is a nation of which the men and women wear the inner bark of a tree sewn together as blanket and general dress. They are born hunters and kill game, even buffaloes, with poisoned arrows. They are also great elephant hunters, which animals they kill with the assegai. As regards their hunting propensities, one can call them the Bushmen of the north side of the Zambesi, but there all likeness ceases, as they are a fine, stalwart, vigorous set of men, very black and great husbandmen, which Bushmen most certainly are not, as they only live from game when they can get it, wild fruit, roots, and general garbage, nothing being amiss or too filthy for them. They are, however, hunters. One great fault, however, which the Manquoia have in common with the Bashukulumbwe is awkward, for anyone being alone or only three or four together are never safe, and it is: they follow your spoor and where they can get you sleeping at night or alone in thick bush so that they can creep on you, they discharge their poisoned arrows at you, with which if they make ever so slight a

---

[1] The Mankoya, a tribe living in the present Mankoya district on the Luena and Luampa rivers, were great hunters and gatherers of wild food. Unlike their neighbours the Mashukulumbwe, they used bows and poisoned arrows.

July, 1886

wound, soon causes death. They then chop off the round top part of the skull, leaving the body exposed to wolves and vultures. This top part of the skull is then cooked, scraped and polished and out of them they drink their beer. Many of them who are now tributary to the Barotse still do it on the sly. The untamed ones take the whole skull and stick them on poles around their towns. On the death of a chief the more heads they can transfix round his grave, the more veneration they show for his memory. We hunt amongst them up the Magelic, but they are always very hospitable and civil to us and provide us with food, no matter how many we be as long as we remain at their village. I expect Dr. Holub will have to pass through some of them. However, I'm not certain which route the natives will take him.

Received letter from Watson, who is getting on very slowly with the house, but why I don't know. Fact is, he's altogether too hasty with natives and understands them very imperfectly.

Returned to my camp on Friday, having shot two quaggas and one gnu. My cook boy and Adonis, who had also arrived, however, got buffalo and shot two ; so now we shall get on for some days. However, as in the hunting veldt I allow them meat ad lib. the amount they have won't last long, as they punish it day and night. Jantje also arrived during my absence on Wednesday, but finding neither meat for himself or boys, started off to look for some. It is now 3.30 P.M. Saturday, but he has not turned up yet. May he shoot something in condition for with the exception of the one quagga there is not enough fat on the five head to grease a gun.

At 5 P.M. had to get under the blankets with a nice dose of the shakes (ague) but was all right again on Sunday, just a little weak. Jantje arrived at 11 A.M., having shot one eland, one sable antelope and two rooi bucks (pallahs). He starts tomorrow S.W. after, or to look for, elephants. Lions roaring all night and they kept up the concert till about 8 A.M., when they were quiet. I think they must have winded us. We have not had a visit from them so close as this morning's yet, though we have come across them twice [when] following game.

Jantje started today and so did I, but my trip was under the blankets again, where I remained until Friday, when I managed to get about again, but very weak. This will put a stop to any sport on my part for some time. One of my boys returned, having shot a buffalo yesterday and on coming to camp for carriers to bring in the meat, shot another, which he covered with bush, only taking out the tongue for my use. Bob also, my pot and kettle carrier, went out yesterday with my Martini Henry (a very light gun), wounded a buffalo, slept in a tree close to the buffalo which he could hear all night, and early in the morning got down from his roost, crept up close to the buffalo and shot it in the ear, killing it at once. (Bob is about fifteen years old and was given to me some years ago by the King, having been taken by him on one of his wars.) And it is the first animal he has ever shot, his former killing having been confined to pheasants and guinea fowls. 'Well done, Bob!' The lad did look pleased as he laid the tongue and tail in front of me and received praise instead of a blowing up, which he knew he had earned by staying out all night as I had only sent him to try and get me a stein buck or orebi, so that I could make some soup. All his mates are, I expect, filled with envy, as Bob is the youngest of the crowd. However, he is as proud as possible, as I have told him to take enough boys to bring the whole of the meat in, and has just given orders to one to make the tail into [a] tsetse fly duster.

Sunday. Sleeping and eating Bob's buffalo. For the boys, I received a present of some grain and tobacco from some outlying natives, which I however more than repaid with meat. All presents from Kafirs with but few exceptions are but sprats to catch the proverbial whale, for they never give without expecting an ample return. It is much cheaper to buy than to receive and it is generally my plan. Of course from chiefs one is bound to accept, though even they expect a return.

Jantje returned today, having made a round of nine days, having seen nothing, not even fresh spoor. He reports having met John Weyers, old and young Klaas, and Gert, who have been in

July, 1886

all directions about Linyanti and not one of them has yet seen an elephant. They are all very much down-hearted, and don't know what to do. Some Bushmen also arrived from Africa, H. Wall and August, they it appears came across a troop of elephants and killed six. Adonis and Skraal as yet have seen nothing. I think I shall send and recall them all and return to our old Magelic veldt, which is now full of elephants bolting from the Barotse who are hunting on the north banks of the Zambesi and Magelic and as my old veldt is without a hunter the elephants are all taking refuge there, so report says. According to native talk, since the veldt has been hunted by the Bushmen for two years and by a number of people from Lake N'gami to whom Luwanika gave permission to hunt, the elephants have been driven through the river. They just come this side but never stay. I am much disappointed, as we always considered the Linyanti the best of hunting veldt, but now it is not worth the trouble of hunting it. I started Jantje today for the Magelic and as soon as I can collect the others shall follow there.

Today is Thursday but I'm not able to go far, being still too weak. A troop of buffaloes came and drank at our pool in the night and I started boys off on spoor in the morning. I also started boys to try and get the hunters together. I shall then propose my plans about the Magelic and I think they will be only too glad. However, if they wish to remain we will do so, though I don't think any will.

Today some people arrived from Mameri,[1] chief of Linyanti, with a request that I would give him some ammunition. I answered his request that as four of my hunters were with him, as soon as I heard that he had shown them where the elephants were, that then I would entertain his modest request ; that ammunition I had and to spare, but that that was the condition on which he would get any. I have known the old fellow for many years and have always known him to be a thorough old humbug and it's a

---

[1] Mamili or Mameri, a Barotse who carried Livingstone's first message to Sebetwane, chief of the Makololo. He lived at Linyanti or had his town in that area after it was deserted, and he was still living in 1899. He was apparently a MuTotela.

fact, my knowledge of which I never try to hide from him, though he can if he will be of great assistance to anyone hunting.

Two o'clock A.M. a troop of buffaloes came to drink at our pool and one of my boys, whose leg had been broken last year by an elephant, becrept them and shot one which turned out to be in good condition. It went away with the troop but dropped dead 100 yds. away from camp, just in the edge of the bush, but the fact of its being dead we did not know till the morning, when we took their spoor from the pool to follow and shoot one. Am having the tongue salted for tomorrow's tit-bit. Wish I could send you some of the eland and buffalo tongues, for you would enjoy them, and I get so many that they are no longer a treat to me. Mameri's people, who are resting here today (the meat being the inducement) say that I must not be down-hearted about the elephants yet although they acknowledge that they are scarcer than they were formerly, but to give the veldt a trial until the warm weather sets in ; that Mameri is sending guides with my people to the elephants' standing-places, known only to themselves, also that until the warm weather commences and the outside waters dry up, they are always scarce but that they come down to the Linyanti River and take to the islands and reeds, only coming out at night and returning at daybreak, but that Mameri will send my boys in after them to do their best. This if true is more reassuring and I will await the attempt, as even if they don't succeed September is quite early enough for the Magelic.

Semansa,[1] a chief living about 20 miles S.E. of this paid me a visit today and brought me about 10 gals. beer as a present. It was very good, and we all enjoyed it. August also sent four boys for a little corn and tobacco, but I had the pleasure of seeing them also carrying two bull tusks which weighed 44 lbs. per tusk and about 20 lbs. good elephant fat, which is our butter and far better than a great quantity of that article. Semansa started home this morning, but has promised that if I send him a couple of hunters he will give

[1] Probably Simonza, a chief whose village was in the bush country about fifteen miles north of the Chobe River and twenty-five miles south of Katima Mulilo Rapids.

July, 1886

them boats and people to follow the elephants into the Masimani Reeds,[1] which are a regular place of refuge for elephants, but without a boat and people to show you about, one is perfectly helpless as the old saying 'looking for a needle in a haystack' goes. It is a great concession if he is not deceiving me, and I have sent for Adonis and one of my Bushmen. May they succeed.

Boys arrived from Weyers today reporting no luck; that W. is going further west, having got boys from Mameri to show him the standing-places, so he sends for the balance of his ammunition which I will send tomorrow.

Adonis arrived today, Monday 27th, having shot a buffalo on his way here which is fat. Game is very scarce here, in fact, without going far and sleeping out, I don't know where to look for it. Wish the outside waters would dry up. However, I went out this morning on eland spoor, which after walking for seven hours on it, brought us within two miles of camp where I saw them standing and made sure of getting one, but I was so puffed with becreeping them through a flat to try and get within shooting distance, that I most completely missed them, and went on to camp thoroughly knocked up and disgusted, and here I shall rest tomorrow and try again on Friday.

But on Friday young Klaas arrived from the Masimani Reeds. He had been in them, but rather too late on Tuesday afternoon, and only saw one cow elephant which he shot but not before they had been well chased by it and having had to take to the water, swimming, and then hiding in the reeds just with his head above water. His gun he had left where he was charged from, as he would have [had] the charge if he had swam with it. When the elephant went back he followed, got his gun and shot it on the spot. It had a young calf. He says the islands are one mass of spoor and quite fresh, so he has not given up hope and says as I do, that there is still plenty of time for the Magelic if they do not succeed here. Mameri has kept his word to me and has given old Klaas, young Klaas and Gert a boat and boatmen each (who know the numerous

---

[1] One of the large reed beds bordering on the Chobe River.

windings through the reeds as well as we know our way about the streets of a town) to be at their command. He has also sent to the outside pools and along the Linyanti west, with directions to the natives who are under him to let him know without delay whenever any elephants put in an appearance, so both I and my people are well pleased.

Today Mameri's son-in-law arrived from their town, bringing me a present of corn. I was very pleased to see him and had a long talk about the veldt. He says there are a good number of elephants amongst the reeds, but wait until the pools dry up and then see. He also brought word to young Klaas that old Klaas was anxious for his return, as they had heard the elephants trumpeting in the reeds the night that he left and wanted to be at them. I sent Mameri a present of 5 lbs. powder, 8 lbs. lead, and one box of 250 percussion caps, which is here a most munificent present, and advising him that everything from me would depend in the future on the reports which young Klaas would send; he on his father's part answering that I should have no cause of complaint, but to just wait and see.

Two lions roaring at the pool all night. It was fine music but a little goes a long way. In the morning I went off to look for elands down a valley where game paths abound, and there came on the spoor of Mr. & Mrs. Leo, which were also going down the same path. Their scent must have driven away all game as they went down wind. After going for about an hour and drawing near the place where I meant to await the elands or any other game that might come to drink, we heard a roar about 50 yards ahead of us. I seized my gun from the bearer, thinking it might be a charge and stood ready for it; but nothing showing we went towards the bush from which the roar had come and saw on the other side the lions trotting off. The male was a magnificent animal and about his front looked almost like a gnu, so black maned was he and so far back did it come over and down his shoulders. The lioness was trotting on in front and though they were a good 400 yds. in front, I let drive and struck up the dust just behind the male, at which I

66

had aimed. Had it been more open, I might have got him, but there was too much fine bush to make a certain shot. The report of the gun quickened them, but not much. However, they got into thick thorn bush and long grass cover, where we left them, thinking discretion the better part of valour. We remained where we were until 2 P.M. but as nothing came to drink we returned to camp, where we found an old Bushman of mine had arrived with meat of a fat buffalo cow, so I smoked my pipe in peace. The two lions came back on our spoor in the night. We heard them at about 8 P.M. giving tongue as they came on, and they kept up the concert at the water all night, joined occasionally by the hyaenas, which had carried off an old quagga skin which we had thrown out as useless. It must have, however, been a rare treat to their insides and feelings, for they were laughing and screaming over it, thinking how they had humbugged us and what a feed they were having. So ended July.

August. Nothing occurred until Thursday, when a buffalo was shot which nearly caught one of my boys. So near was it that as he was trying to get into a tree it struck him with its nose, its horns luckily bending too far back to strike him with them. Finding he was out of reach, it came three times full tilt at the tree, thinking to shake him down, and as it was so engaged and butting the tree, one of the others crept close up from tree to tree and shot it with an elephant gun through the shoulders.

On Friday a Kafir arrived from Molemwa, one of my old boatmen of Sepopa's days, who had come from the King with orders to turn me out of the Linyanti veldt[1] and that I must at once return to the Magelic as that country belonged to me and no other. I was both surprised and angry that Luwanika had made such a fool of me. However, I told the Kafir I did not believe him, and that the word Luwanika had given me, that I should go and no other and that I would send to Shesheki and find out the truth, but if Molemwa had a message from the King to that effect his place was to come and deliver it.

---

[1] Which Lewanika kept as an elephant preserve for himself.

No. 59

Over the Zambesi. July 27th 1875

The assagai in the buffalo's back has not made him more friendly. One of the Africans has climbed a large termite heap to get out of the way.

Nos. 62 and 63

At Sejoro. N. of Zambesi.
Door in Palisade. and Hut in Kaffir Kraal. Zambesi

The palisading was made by planting a row of upright stakes five feet or so apart and fastening reeds to the cross-poles. The door looks as if it were secured by a log.

The Barotse built several kinds of huts. In this type, there was an inner structure, high and cone-shaped, with its separate vaulted roof; this was surrounded by a lower cylindrical wall supporting a conical roof. The outer doorway was rectangular, as shown here, or semioval, like the inner one. Sometimes the outer roof was extended five or six feet beyond its wall and the extension was supported by posts to form a verandah.

Sejoro is a corruption of the name *Jolosi Mulite*, a village in the Machili Valley and situated today about twenty-one miles northeast of Mwandi on the Zambezi.

No. 59

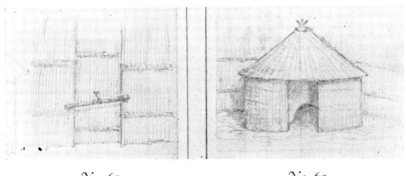

No. 62 No. 63

No. 65

No. 66

No. 65

Thatching a House—Sesheke

This operation is performed in the same way today. Women cut the long, dry thatching grass in the veld and tie it into bundles eight to twelve inches in diameter. These are laid together in rows on the roof framework and combed into a uniform, interlacing whole of about the same thickness as the bundles. From the sketch it would seem that the division of labour in the tribe put this task in the domain of the women.

No. 66

The King's House. Sesheke

Sipopa had three huts for himself inside a fenced enclosure of oval shape. There were several smaller buildings of various kinds for storing medicines, assagais, elephant tusks and tails, and other miscellanea, and in one of them the royal occupant bathed in a large wooden tub. One side of the King's enclosure was bounded by the Zambezi, and surrounding it were three more concentric fences, the nearest enclosing the dwellings of his wives, the next containing the storehouse, kitchens, and musicians' quarters, and the last the huts of the servants.

On Sunday Molemwa came and greeted me kindly and I at once opened the ball by asking him for an explanation of his messenger's meaning. 'Oh,' he said, 'the man has heard or dreamt of something, I suppose, and as I only sent him to advise you of my arrival, thought it would show a little authority on his part if he had something to say. The King's message is this. Go to where you hear Joros (my name) is, and tell him how things are with me, and about Moremi, and ask him why he was in such a hurry to hunt in the Linyanti. If he had first with his hunters have gone to the Magelic and my hunters to the Zambesi rapids and there warmed up the elephants in those parts, then when the weather got warm they could have crossed through into the Linyanti and would have found plenty of elephants which had taken refuge from the guns of my hunters at the rapids and his on the Magelic. However, as I was now here, I must just do as best I could.' I thanked Molemwa and told him that as the King had also given permission to Moremi, Chief of Lake N'gami to hunt the Linyanti, I thought we might find on arrival here that he had killed and driven out what we also wanted, and that was the only reason we came straight here. 'You were quite right,' said Molemwa, 'and the King will understand, but it's no use my telling him anything, for when you two are together, you are just like man and wife, so you can tell him yourself.'

'However, the friendship that existed between Moremi and Luwanika is broken, for on Moremi's way home after parting from Luwanika and after our King presenting him with so many people and cattle, he gave over the people [of] a town [of] Mambugushu[1] belonging to Luwanika to be murdered by his followers. They were all killed, only their headman escaping and he has since died from grief. Thus that friendship is broken and the only one that both we his people and himself called friend is yourself? (Flattery) But then you are a Marotse and our father, and were you not Sepopa's friend and is Luwanika [not] more your child on that account? So don't think that Moremi will interfere with your

[1] Mampukushu. See note 2, page 45.

August, 1886

hunting, as he will not be allowed to cross the river.' So ended our talk and on Monday Molemwa started to cross through to the north bank of the Zambesi with a number of Bushmen whom he has in charge to shoot elephants for the King. May he be successful and warm them so well up that they may cross to this side and we get our share of them here.

Had a letter from Watson saying that April's elephant bull weighed 85 and 87 lbs. in the two tusks, and that April, Andries and Jantje will hunt in the Magelic. Sent out the Manquoia to hunt for honey and I went in another direction to look for game. As they went down the valley close to camp they came across three lions which had pulled down and killed a buffalo heifer. They drove away the lions and took the meat, for there was still more than half the buffalo left, and were still standing there when they heard bellowing about 200 yds. ahead of them. They ran in the direction and saw a fine male lion trying to pull down another buffalo, which was giving tongue for assistance, and it soon came for the whole troop came back at the charge and Mr. Leo was obliged to leave his little game unfinished and the subject went off with the troop, the lion following and my boys also took up the spoor. But the buffaloes were too wary now for the lion to make another venture, for every now and then some old bulls would turn round and force His Majesty to retreat. This species of tactic took place for some distance, so the boys returned to where they had left the first meat with one of their comrades and returned to camp with it. I also returned late in the evening, having seen nothing but an orebi at which I did not shoot, and on the boys reporting their luck was very disappointed at having missed such a chance at both lions and buffaloes. Such is luck. Semansa paid me another visit on Thursday and with another lot of beer which was again enjoyed by us all.

On the 13th boys arrived from Africa and Henry Wall with two good bull tusks and sixteen cow ditto. They are going further to the N.W. having been out to inspect the veldt as far as Umtembanya's.[1]

---

[1] Matambanje's. See note 2, page 34.

On the road having met a troop of tuskers and killed the bull and eight cows. They sent me word that there is no lack of elephant spoor where they were and they are now off for that place.

August and J. P. Weyers have gone up along the Zambesi and are nearly opposite the Gonye Falls. They will take spoor going west into the middle veldt between the Zambesi and Linyanti (Chobe is another name for the Linyanti River) rivers. Expect to hear from August soon.

The Manquoia came across two lions that I saw about two weeks ago. They had come across and killed a buffalo cow that I had broken the leg of two days ago. They had not killed it long, as the meat was still warm, but had torn it open and taken out certain parts. It is a strange fact and no hunter's yarn that when a lion kills any game and is undisturbed that he takes out the leaf, paunch and other particular parts which he buries close to where he has killed the game. It is, to people unaware of the fact, almost incredible, but perfectly true, and Bushmen always look out for the buried parts and take them up. They call it the lion's medicine, by which he insures good luck.[1]

On the 18th shot a buffalo cow which we saw with her calf away from the herd. I broke her hind leg and she came for us, but took after the boys, who were soon up trees. I also had my tree ready, but was only behind it ready for a quick ascent. It stood looking at the boys not 20 yards from me and being broadside on and a good shot I gave it a bullet with a 12 bore Whitworth through the shoulder blade. It started forward a couple of yards and then dropped dead, and the boys to show their pluck commenced assegaing it, which I, however, soon stopped. Sent out the boys on Saturday but they returned empty handed.

On Monday 23rd started boys carrying elephant fat and buffalo marrow to Watson. It is six days journey from here but I am

---

[1] Lions first lick up the blood about and on a carcass, then they disembowel it and lay the paunch some short distance off; then they empty the paunch and scrape earth and leaves over the contents. This is almost always done, and the reason for it is not known. (J. Stevenson-Hamilton, *Wild Life in South Africa*, London, 1947, p. 147.)

anxious for news. Hear that the new Maransian has arrived at Shesheki with all his petty chiefs and others from the King to take the places of those who have been killed. Also he has three of the King's 'big men' with him to act as councillors to him, [he] being still very young for the position and he is only 16 or 17 years old, but he is Naqwi's the Queen of Nalolo's son, thus being nephew to Luwanika is of greater importance than any other would be. All the dependents of the tribes big and little subject to Shesheki and who have to take their tribute to that town have been called up Sho-ellella. We have no English meaning for the word, but you will be pretty near the meaning by using the words : offering, thanks and praise, and asking for peace, or as they say, sleep.

Out again today but saw nothing but a duiker which was very close to me but at which I would not shoot, thinking I might drive away bigger game that might be close to me. Sorry afterwards I did not bag it, as I returned to camp empty handed and it would have been a certain supper.

On the 25th a man arrived from Shesheki having been sent by the chiefs of that town with a message purporting to have been sent by the King, although they themselves had only just arrived and had received no personal message from the King. Still, this is it.

Joros must at once collect his people and leave the Linyanti country which the King never gave him but which he is stealing, and he must come via Shesheki, so that we can see him and receive the ivory which he has shot, the Magelic being his but not the Linyanti. This man met my boys carrying the fat etc. to Watson so they returned with him. I was too confused to give the man any answer and he himself can't understand it, for he says, 'How can such a message come from the King when we all know that the country has been given to you? If it is true, who can believe the Barotse after this, and you, the King's friend?' However, I have started two of my boys to Shesheki for I can't believe it, not that I particularly care about Linyanti but I am sorry and angry that the King can be such a liar, and that he could have

73

No. 67

Houses in Sesheke

These hemispherical, concentric huts were built by the Masubia, a riverine tribe subject to the Barotse. They lived on the lower Chobe and on the Zambezi upwards some distance from the mouth of the Chobe.

No. 68

A Doctor. Sesheke

One of the Masubia witchdoctors who danced at Sesheke. His headdress of wildebeest or zebra tails and apron of skins ornamented with similar tails are shown, besides his gourd rattles and dancing mat.

No. 67

No. 68

№. 69

№. 70

No. 69

Doctors. Sesheke

The Masubia doctors danced this prophetic dance in pairs for hours, sometimes for a whole day ; when they collapsed with exhaustion, they prophesied for the King about royal projects such as raids. They performed by hopping about and varied their dance occasionally by dropping to the ground or sinking gradually. The headdresses of both have come off in this sketch.

No. 70

Zambesi. The King Paddling

Sipopa keeping his hand in as a boatman, in a canoe with very little freeboard. The solar topee, checked shirt, and waistcoat are evidence of his fondness for European clothing.

made such a tool of me, but I'm in the hands of the Philistines and must try to bear it patiently. How to get my boys together, I don't know, for neither my boys nor myself know where some of them are, so I shall still let them hunt 'aphazard,' but I have sent word to Shesheki that if the report is true that they can send people to look for them themselves. In spite of all bad news one must eat, so I went out and shot an eland bull and one of my boys shot a buffalo bull and a calf with one bullet, the bullet going through the bull and also killing the calf which was standing a few paces off on the other side. So we had plenty of meat.

Received letters from Watson, Dr. Holub and Lobengula (Matabele King), the latter having been written by Fairbairn. Watson's has no news, except that nothing has been done yet towards building the new house. It seems he can't get boys. Dr. H.'s came from Mapansa's,[1] a Matoka chief on the outskirts of Bashulumbwe. His journey has, as I always imagined, been abruptly brought to an end by the Bashukulumbwe, who robbed him of everything and killed one of his Austrian servants,[2] and he had to beg his way back, fever-stricken, from town to town. I'm very, very sorry for him, but especially so for his poor wife, though we can only be surprised at their miraculous escape, for a miracle it is. He had to take to shooting in self-defence and shot three niggers, which had the effect of making them cautious and so [he] escaped. I have not heard all particulars yet but hope to soon. I am too far off here to render him any assistance, but I am sure that Watson will do so and do all he possibly can for their comfort. As soon as the rain falls I will gladly lend them a wagon and oxen to take them south, but at present travelling is impossible unless to one who knows the country thoroughly for water, and the Dr. does not. The Dr. and his poor wife have not even a blanket to cover them and no change of clothing, they and their two surviving servants have not a complete pair of boots amongst them.

---

[1] At or near Mapanza Mission, 16° 15′ south latitude and 26° 55′ east longitude, about halfway between the Kafue and the Zambezi in a north-south line.

[2] Oswald Zoldner was the Austrian servant who was killed.

August, 1886

The males are compelled to wear native sandals and are terribly footsore and blistered. Mrs. H. has one shoe and one top boot, and added to this, hunger and fever are busy with them and they are entirely without medicine. Had the Dr. not taken to shooting they would all excepting Mrs. H. have been murdered, and she to a white woman would have had a fate worse than death, for she would have been the slave of the one who captured her and entirely at his will. Of course, I should have gone and rescued her (or tried to) with my hunters, but only think how she would have suffered before any rescue could have got to her. I expect a fair quantity of niggers would have bitten the dust before we should have been satisfied, for we have not all Christian feelings, neither are we all saints, and I know my hunters would have been animated by their master and he most certainly is *not* a saint or would not have been in this case, and we are pretty well known, our hunting veldt extending up to the Bashukulumbwe river of Luengi,[1] the other side of which the Dr. met with his mishap.

Fairbairn's from Lobengula is greetings from His Majesty and thanking me for a present of monkey and black civet cat skins that I made him. Some three years ago he gave Phillips, Leask, Fairbairn and myself Baines' concessions of the Mashonaland Gold Fields,[2] and we have sent in an experienced practical miner to see them, report and bring samples of the quartz. Phil has gone there, hope it may turn up trumps, for in these times of dull and no trade something is wanting. F. writes that on the Matabele country they are doing literally nothing.

[1] Another name for the Kafue River.

[2] Westbeech, Fairbairn, and Thomas Leask, an ex-elephant hunter and then a storekeeper at Klerksdorp, Transvaal, signed an agreement before witnesses at Klerksdorp on 3 June 1881. They agreed to approach Lobengula to obtain mining and mineral rights, and to take Phillips, who was absent, into their syndicate. After much delay, Loben signed, at Bulawayo on 25 January 1884, a concession giving them leave to mine gold in Mashonaland between the Gwelo and the Hunyani rivers. Another grant (both were negotiated by Phillips and Fairbairn) covering all the country controlled by the Matabele was obtained on 14 July 1888. After much bargaining, Leask in 1889 sold them to Rhodes's agents for the Chartered Company for about £20,000, a fourth of which was paid to Westbeech's estate. Thomas Baines, the artist-explorer, was given in 1871 the first concession to the Mashonaland Goldfields.

No. 71

The King's Children at Sesheke

The boy on the left is practising throwing the assagai with a reed as substitute. The girl is developing skill at carrying objects on her head, a thing Bantu women are very good at and are trained to from an early age ; that she must steady it with her hand shows that she is still learning.

No. 72

Women Stamping Corn—Sesheke

They are making coarse meal of maize (mealies) or kaffir corn (non-saccharin sorghums) by alternating their blows. The mortar and pestles are wooden, the method is common to all the Bantu tribes, though a smaller mortar and short pestle, better suited to one female operator, were more usual ; or the grain might also be ground between two stones.

No. 71

No. 72

No. 73

No. 75

No. 73

Boys Spearing Fish–Zambesi

They are in reedy shallows, where crocodiles are more easily guarded against and the fish more easily taken. Fishing is most commonly practised as the flood waters recede, when the mouths of tributaries and creeks can be dammed and the fish secured by spearing and in basket traps.

No. 75

The King Drinking Honey Beer

Sipopa has discarded his European clothes and is wearing a blanket. The drink is made from fermented wild honey, which men were sent to gather in the veld. The place is the interior of a royal hut, with one of his wives on the King's right and his cup-bearer, Matungulu, pouring from a large gourd with a twisted neck that serves as a spout. The tin mug was a present from West-beech, and another article of European make, a glass tumbler, is shown.

September 1st. Boys returned from Shesheki, but from their report am very little wiser. On the road they met Sekosi, Chief of Katongo, where I crossed the river on the way here. He was surprised at the news, for he is the last arrival from the King and had heard nothing about such things. However, I shall take the ivory and go to Shesheki, that they can do as they desire, and then try and get a boat, start for the Barotse [Valley] and have it out with the King.

Shot two buffaloes yesterday late in the afternoon and as we had no time to carry the meat away, left them lying where they fell until this morning. During the night the lions came and entirely finished one, only leaving the marrow bones and tongue, so we only got the meat of the other and lucky we were to get even that.

On the 3rd started the boys with some of the things for the river, whence they return tomorrow night. Will then be able to manage the return loads and start with them myself to where they left the first lot, then try and get a boat from Sekosi to transport the ivory etc. to Shesheki, which three boys can row while I walk with the others, it only being about 50 miles from Katongo, so I'll manage that easily in two days.

I cannot realise that this message is from the King, for as the natives say, I cannot understand that one in whom is vested all the power and who could have as easily refused the hunting veldt as he willingly gave it, can have two hearts. However, we shall see and as I hear from the boys, some of his chiefs are as confounded as I am, especially my old friends Ra Touw (Father of Lions) and Magumpa.

Sept. 5th. My birthday today. Started with the boys who had returned from where they had deposited the first loads. I left Impatcha at 7 A.M. and at 5 P.M. called a halt to make sleeping places. Whilst the boys were at this work, went out and shot a pallah (rooi buck) so we had fresh meat. Must have done close on thirty miles today for we stuck to it well, through the bush, no footpaths, sun so hot that my feet were blistered and it was not a happy birthday. However, I only felt sore, not a bit tired.

THE DIARY OF GEORGE WESTBEECH

Arrived at the loads at 9 A.M. on the 6th in the afternoon. Shot a sea-cow (hippopotamus) and puku (no English name, only found about the Zambesi, where they are plentiful), nearly all the meat of which I gave to the poor natives living about, which would keep the wolf from the door a few days. All the niggers about here are slaves and have nothing they may call their own.

Next afternoon off for the river, which is only seven miles from this. Here I found Sekosi at home, who insists on taking me to Shesheki himself per boat, for which I am truly grateful, so kept three boys with me and sent the others ahead to that town, where they arrived next day. All was done as arranged and on arrival at Shesheki went at once to the kothla (council square)[1] where I found the new Maransian and all his chiefs assembled. Had a long talk with them and told them that as the Linyanti was never given me by Luwanika I did not want any difference of opinion, neither would I argue with them, and as they also said it was their intention to take any ivory I might have I had brought them twenty-two tusks and they had better send people to take them away from my camp, that their value in my sight after having been made a liar by themselves and the King was nil.

I then left them there and the next morning started off my boys (retaining three) for Gazungula, but stayed myself, having borrowed a boat from Maransian. In the afternoon I went to them again and told them that as I was going to make an early start they had better take away the ivory for I should leave it lying where it was. Then they asked me why I had not sent on the ivory with my boys, as it was mine. I told them as yesterday, that it had no more value in my eyes, that (and here I think I acted as a first-class diplomatist) I had lived with them for fifteen years but this was the first time I had ever been called liar and thief by them or any other tribe, that I was intimate [with] and the friend of many chiefs, but theirs was the first that when he gave a thing did it with two mouths, that I had assisted him and them in many

[1] Sechuana *kxotla,* Lozi *Kuta,* an enclosure where tribal meetings were held and where other business was transacted.

81

troubles and had kept their drifts free from Matabele through my
friendship with that King [Lobengula] whose no was NO and yes
was YES. That I should now return only to Mamboowa to my old
friend Magumpa, get his people and big boat and start at once for
the valley, just to say goodbye to their King and return him his
false friendship and all further care of his drifts; that I should
leave them and return to the country given me many years ago by
the Matabele King and which was still mine, but as a last advice
to them I told them they had better get someone who was as much
a friend of the Matabele as I was, to be their friend with that King.
This turned the tables at once. Who should they get to be their
eyes and ears on the Matabele side of the river, or who knew or
was trusted by that King as I was? Oh no! we can't part with you.
Why, when you first came among us our children who are parents
now, were the children themselves, and they know that Luwanika
had given me the Linyanti and was acting childishly and they
certainly could not think of taking anything belonging to me.
'Part with Joros? What nonsense, etc.' I told them it was all right
and they could get someone in whom they had more faith than in
me to watch over their interest, but I was tired of being made a
tool and fool of. Well, they would not even go and look at the
ivory, but in the night sent a big boat and oarsmen to convey it to
a new place at Gazungula. Their own boys (slaves) told me that
night sitting at the fire that had they not been afraid of the Matabele if I left them, that they meant to take the ivory. This I knew
very well, so made no comment.

Got to Gazungula on Wednesday, stayed one day with Watson
(house started on) and on Friday started back with Magumpa's
big boat and eight rowers for the valley (not much rest for poor
me), not even a servant of my own with me, and here I am today at
Gatima Molelo Rapids.[1] Got through them and the others with

---

[1] Katima Mulilo (Put-Out-the-Fire) Rapids, the first above Sesheke and the first of
a series of about twenty-four rapids on the Zambezi that extend for eighty miles. This
is a slight fall, full of rocks and boulders; canoes can be poled through them if the
water is low enough. Site of the present Government station of Sesheke.

September–October, 1886

great trouble, having to drag the boat through the shallows and over the rocks, and after eleven hours hard rowing and hauling from Gatima Molelo (Put Out the Fire) arrived at N'gambwe Cataract (here's where I got that cheering post last year) on Sunday 26th September in the evening, but too tired, and so were the boys, to even attempt to make a sleeping place, a thing that is never omitted, so just lay down under a tree on, or rather close to, the bank and went supperless to bed, for I and they were too fagged even to eat, though we had food enough.

Next day tried to get the boat pulled round the cataract, but failed, being short-handed, so sent to collect (or try to) people to assist. Here I shot a spur winged goose and pallah and one of the boatmen wounded a buffalo. Very unwell in the evening ; feeling more fit for a sick bed than travelling to the Barotse in an open boat and sick or well having to look for game to feed my men. Took two big doses of quinine ; made a kettle of tea which I took at intervals as hot as I could drink it and got under the blankets, though the sun must have been considerably more than 100 in the shade. Very cloudy this evening, expect we shall have rain soon, which will be far from pleasant. Well, I was not kept very long in suspense for it rained nearly all night. Got the boat dragged and carried round next morning and made another start. Chased in the afternoon by a sea-cow, but after a couple of shots it gave up the chase.

After several detentions, having to re-sew the boat, after getting through every rapid, got to Seoma (Gonye Cataract) on Sunday 3rd October, though had all gone well ought to have got here on Thursday or Friday. Monday and Tuesday [was] collecting people to carry and pull the boat round the cataract, a distance of about four miles, and off again on Wednesday 6th. After much boat mending, we arrived at Nalolo, the Queen Muguwi's place on Monday 11th. Here stayed one day to visit her, and got to the King's on the 14th. Such has been the heat of the sun that from Seoma I had to make a small tent from a native net over my sitting place in the boat. Although I can stand a pretty hot bake oven, still this October sun has been too much even for me.

October, 1886

Since leaving Shesheki have passed 127 hippos, shot two and been chased twice. I shot also 23 spur winged geese, 28 mongollas, a black bird about twice the size of a duck and capital eating,[1] eight ducks and one pallah, so we have not starved, though as soon as you enter the valley it is very difficult to get anything to shoot and that is where birds were so acceptable.

Found the King very well and fat and very glad to see me. Took up my quarters as usual with the Prime Minister and on the quiet had a long talk to him about the reports I had been continually hearing in the hunting field. He says, 'You know the King. Yes, he is King? But at present he has to do his best to please [the] Barotse, and reports kept arriving that you had killed all the elephants in the veldt, and his hunters generally returned unsuccessful or only having killed one elephant, which caused jealousy, so he sent word that you were to return to your old ground of Magelic, but not that what you had shot had to be taken from you, those reports being circulated by the messengers ; however, I should hear everything from His Majesty.' I told him in reply that I was sick of the whole affair of their nation generally, that my only wish now was to say goodbye and leave their country. This did not prove pleasant news at all, for he said, 'We cannot part with you! However, you will hear the King.' This after several days patience I did.

He confirms all that the Prime Minister said, acknowledging that he gave me the Linyanti, but his people being dissatisfied he had to give way to them. He, however, thought that as he had not gone to the hunt himself, that I would have gone to the Magelic and not have hunted the Linyanti until we went together. I answered, 'If such had been your wish, why did you not let me know when you sent down the ivory to trade in June, and I could not have gone to the Linyanti.' He said he should have done so but did not think about it. Thus ended the talk, except that we must

---

[1] The African openbill stork (*Anastomus lamelligerus*), a black and brown bird of the upper Zambezi marshes that is about thirty inches long. It is called *nongolo* today, and the name Westbeech uses may be a corruption of the old Lozi name.

October, 1886

be satisfied as we had shot a lot of elephants and his people nothing ; that what I had was mine and he never gave orders to either
Shesheki people or anyone else that my ivory was to be taken away,
only that I was to return to the Magelic (and I don't believe him a
little bit ! !). I thanked him ; said had I known that the Linyanti
was so shot out I would not have hunted one day in it ; that the
Magelic was a much larger and better country (though it's only
larger, but not half so good).

Another day he began telling me of all the benefits he had con-
ferred upon me by giving me hunting country, and went on at a
great rate until quite dry. I quietly listened. When he was quiet I
asked him if he was quite done and then began to tell him what I
had done for and given him since he had been made King, and as a
wind up I told him that I was not aware that he had put the elephants in a compound for me, nor tied them fast, neither had I
heard that he had sent out his supreme orders that on my approach
the elephants had to drop tusks as a snake sheds its skin, and clear
off, but that I had laboured under the ignorant and erroneous im-
pression that all the elephants we had shot had been by much hard
walking and perspiring, but I begged his pardon for my foolish
mistake, and in future when we shot an elephant should render
thanks and all praise to him for his generous assistance in giving
us walking power enough to catch it up. But perhaps it might be
as well for us to break our friendship now, as I saw we were tired
of each other. I then got up and went to my hut, leaving him to
ruminate. In the evening he sent for me to go and drink honey
beer. Went, and found him very pleasant. After a little he asked
me what had made me tell him off as I had done in the morning ;
to which I answered that as there was neither honesty in himself
or [his] people I was sick of the whole lot, and indeed I had only
come to say goodbye.

After a little silence he said, 'No, I will never agree to your
leaving me, but want to bring a couple of your wagons to the
valley and trade with me personally as you did with Sepopa (chief
when I first arrived in the country in 1871), to bring my hunters

No. 76

One of Sepopa's Wives having a Bath–Zambesi

To enter any of these rivers to bathe would have been to risk being taken by a crocodile, so bathing was done on the land.

No. 79

Columns of Spray rising from the Victoria Falls–Decr–1875

The spray cloud is visible at from six to thirty miles away, depending on the volume of water in the river.

Nᵒ. 76

Nᵒ. 79

No. 80

No. 99

No. 80

Our Camp 8 miles from Victoria Falls. Dec. 1875

MacLeod's party never reached the Falls, because they were twice stopped close to them by fever. This sketch and the one immediately preceding it are souvenirs of the first attempt, in early December, when Fairlie was with the others. Biltong, strips of meat dried in the air and sun with or without salt, is curing in front of the temporary grass hut.

No. 99

A Night in the Bush. 21st Novr. 75. Near Gashumba. Zambesi

One of the party has been unable to find his way back to camp and has been forced to spend the night out, sleeping with his saddle as a pillow and near a fire for protection against lions and other prowlers. The place is in or near the Khazuma Flat, on the road from Pandamatenga to the junction of the Chobe and Zambezi rivers.

October–November, 1886

also and they could hunt for me anywhere, that when I was with him he felt safer from the Barotse and that I could live where I liked in the country.' Happy lot, his position as King of the Barotse? But as I said before I don't believe him, [and] just answered that I would think about it, and we spent a pleasant evening.

Mr. Coillard has arrived in the valley with his wagons, after much trouble [and] has been two months on the road. He returns soon to Shesheki to get Mrs. C. before the country becomes flooded and impassable.[1] The King has taken to him but the people want to know what he wants there, and he won't trade with them and they want to know nothing about the white man's book, as by learning *it* they can only have one wife, and where are they then going to get beer? I expect it will go hard with him yet, as I don't believe one little bit in the nation amongst whom he has cast his lot. If the King were only secure *as* King, it might go well, but Luwanika can be deposed and murdered at any time, and then it's a reign of 'anyone take what's not too hot or too heavy' for them.

Stayed at the King's until 31st Oct. when I left and spent the 1st Nov. at Sola (Sepopa's old town)[2] to kill an ox and dry the meat for the journey. Got to Queen Muguwi's on the 2nd, who killed another ox for me. Here I was again prostrated with fever and had to remain until the 6th when I left, and after enjoying in my weak state the benefit of being wet all day from rains which have now set in, arrived at Gonye Falls on the 9th and after getting boats dragged and carried round the falls, got started again on the 12th though not till late, as we had again to begin boat mending. After half a day's hard pulling we got to Matomwai's village at the head of the Kali Rapids.[3] Here I received a present of a decent lot of corn and ground nuts, which was very acceptable as my boys

---

[1] Coillard, Middleton, and Waddell, the latter a Scots artisan, brought their three ox wagons to Sefula, their new station, on 11 October 1886. Coillard fetched his wife up from Sesheke in canoes by 10 January 1887.

[2] Apparently the village Sipopa used as a residence when in the Barotse Valley.

[3] See note 1, page 43. The Kali Rapids below the Gonye Falls. Matome's was above the Kali; then come the Nangula Fall, the Sitamba Rapids, then the Gonye.

November, 1886

were completely out of food, as up to the present, excepting geese shot coming through the valley, have not seen a single head of game. Bought a boat of Matomwai and his boys row me in it to receive payment. Arrived at N'gambwe Cataract on the 14th and went next morning to look for buffaloes, but not seeing any, started next morning for Katongo, where we arrived at 5.30 P.M. after shooting a sea-cow and two geese. The boys stood to the oars well for nine and a half hours ; the only stay being made was to take about 5 cwt. of the meat and present the balance of about 3,000 lbs. (it was a full grown cow) to some river niggers living close by, to whom it was a godsend. Another nine hours good pulling took us to Shesheki next day, and the following morning I went down to the town, got the chiefs together and told them the King's answer about taking the ivory shot by us at Linyanti. They were *very tame* and answered that it was just as they thought, though the report had reached them to take everything from me, but they would take steps to punish those who had brought false reports, which I may as well tell you is all moonshine. I also told them that perhaps it was as well they did not try force, as something else might have remained on the ground besides ivory, and there might have been a few less beer drinkers in their town. Thus ended the Linyanti news.

I left Shesheki the same day at 12.30 and got to where the Magelic flows into the Zambesi. Here we had to make the best sleeping places we could out of a few mats, not waterproof as the grass had all been burnt off and the rain coming down per buckets full or as some say 'like old boots.' In the rain shot a leche buck, and making an early start next morning, being chased by a sea-cow with calf at Cachila, got to Momboowa at 2 P.M. where I slept, but sick again, I suppose from yesterday's wet clothes, and next morning at 9 A.M. arrived at Gazungula, where I found the new house only just begun, Watson well, and an old friend Tom Fry[1]

[1] A hunter and trader who was at the Zambezi and visited the Victoria Falls in 1877. He returned downcountry to John Lee's in Matabeleland during October to December and went on to Tati, where he lingered till February 1878 before going out.

also there, who had arrived from Mangwato in October with a load of goods for sale. These I took over, provided wagon and ten oxen for Dr. Holub and also for my own transport and on December 7th started Watson for Klerksdorp, where he arrived some time in March, having been detained by rain nearly the whole road. All the oxen he had, and those I lent to Dr. Holub, died on the road, and they had to get assistance to arrive in Mangwato. Here was a great loss to me again, as all the oxen had to be replaced to enable Watson to continue his journey. Nearly all of Fry's also died.

Well, by this time I'm beginning to believe that I shall never be lucky again. I stayed at the Zambesi instead of going south, very ill and weak, and although so sick continued building and superintending those that built and on the 16th January was able to move into the new house; also had vegetable garden made and tried to make myself as comfortable as possible.

On the 6th March came on vomiting blood (I suppose from the liver) which left me frightfully weak, and not being very strong before, it took me a long time to pull round. However, with what care I was able to take of myself (only having natives about me) and plenty of green food, I got on pretty well, and when the wagons arrived in June, I was fit again. Watson brought two gentlemen to cross the river and do some hunting. The permission for this I got easily for them, as the country they would hunt in (Magelic) belongs to me, that is, it's my hunting ground granted by the Barotse.

I now made ready for going to the Barotse Valley per wagon to open up the country and to do or try to do some trading with the King. Crossed wagon, oxen and goods through the Zambesi and on the 22nd July said goodbye to Starkey and Cory (the two gentlemen)[1] at Mamboowa, they proceeding to hunt, I to the

[1] John R. Starkey and his friend Cory picked up Frank Watson at Mafeking in April 1887. Watson was taking two wagon loads of goods to Westbeech, who obtained leave for them to shoot and sent one of his experienced elephant hunters with them as guide and mentor. Starkey, Cory, and Watson left the Zambezi on 5 September and made Shoshong in forty-three days.

July–October, 1887

valley, when I passed the night in a mud hole. With Starkey I sent a warm and large otter kaross to my cousin. I could write you a lot about my journey to the valley, but it was so entirely without interest that it would be monotonous. However, it took me from the 22nd July till 6th September before I arrived at the King's as the cattle were most wretchedly poor, one dying from poverty on the road, there being literally nothing for the poor beasts to eat, so at the Injoko River I started collecting carriers to assist from river to river, and had not much difficulty, putting it down as King's work and King's goods, and wherever they began to grumble, I used just to call up the cattle, load off the loads and leave them, knowing they would soon be following my trail, though I should not advise a stranger to try the same plan. Well, I started by getting 24 carriers and ended by arriving in the valley with 65, so that I was able to assist the poor cattle considerably. Had I not have adopted that plan, I should never have arrived in the valley. King very pleased at my arrival and on the 8th commenced making an enclosure round the wagon, around which he put coloured reed mats, which seen from a little distance had a very pleasing effect. It's called the King's Compound, so I'm pretty free from outsiders. On the 5th October the King started leche buck hunting, promising to be back in fourteen days, has also been daily sending off hunters to try and shoot elephants.

J. Stromboom,[1] one of the traders from Lake N'gami, arrived on the 17th October to see what he could do with Luwanika in the

---

[1] John Stromboom, a British subject of Scandinavian ancestry, was born in Oslo Norway, about 1843. He came to Natal in 1862, and in the same year proceeded with G. A. Phillips to the Transvaal and worked at a store in Pretoria. About 1864 Stromboom went to Lake Ngami to trade, and he made four more journeys there; then he tried his luck at Kimberley, but returned to Ngamiland in 1873. He had great influence with the Tawana tribe and became a headman. He was consulted by the chief Lechulatebe in affairs of state, and when that chief died Stromboom was made guardian to his young heir, Moremi II. This made the trader prime minister in all but name and first advisor to the new chief. He obtained a mineral, grazing, and timber concession in the Ngami country in 1889, and died at Mafeking in 1893. He was the Westbeech of the Tawana.

On this journey, Stromboom went from Lealui, 200 miles up the Zambezi and Kabompo rivers, to see Lewanika.

way of trading for ivory, he having left his wagons at my place Gazungula. However, the King being still away, he left on the 7th Nov. to see His Majesty in the hunting veldt, which was only three days distant, he, J.S., being anxious to return south. If the King does not return soon, I shall not be able to get to Gazungula before the winter, as the rivers will prevent me. Delightful country. Shall let him know my opinion of him pretty freely on his return, as he had promised to be away only fourteen days.

On the 25th November the Grand Mukamuk returned and we did have words, a few, that is, he said nothing, as he could not, his only excuse being that the game excited him and he kept hunting. He with his dogs and people (for it was a succession of surrounds, native way of hunting) killed over seven hundred mache (plural for leche) bucks, so it *was* exciting enough for him though it delayed me, as it was all assegai work, no guns being permitted ; that is why I had not gone with him as I did with Sepopa, the old King, in 1874, when we did it with boats, natives driving the game down to the valley from the high lands, when we would chase them with boats in shallow water. In Sepopa's hunt I shot thirty-seven head and had a pleasant time of it, during which we also killed over seven hundred head, but then we got a lion, a tiger,[1] also elands and gnus, besides mache, and although Luwanika's hunt had a lion in it, they did not get it, but it got one of his boys and got off scot free.

Stromboom returned south on the 27th November having only received four bull tusks for a horse, seventy lbs. ivory for a breech-loader and one tusk for a present, worth about half as much as the present he gave the Grand Mukamuk.

28*th*. Received a fine ox for slaughter, which was very acceptable, also bought 23 tusks, which was much more acceptable, and as by 6th December all my goods were done, I left the valley and after much rain and in consequence much mud and hard work, arrived at Shesheki on the 27th, Inquesi [River] on the 1st January 1888, but which was flooded ; however I got boats from

[1] Leopard.

92

January, 1888

my old friend Magumpa, took wagon again to pieces and ferried it and everything through and swam the oxen across. This was on the 3rd and then I went on to Mamboowa per boat, wagon arrived night of the 4th. It was only four hours journey from Inquesi to Mamboowa (Magumpa's town) but owing to the mud it took them over two days. Here I killed an ox given me by Magumpa and went by boat one and a half hours to Gazungula on the 5th where I found everything all right, but the boys short of food, Watson not having left them sufficient when he left on the 5th of September, thinking I should not have been so long absent.

On the 6th came on again that blood vomiting of last year, and I lost so much that Middleton[1] who was with me, gave up all hope. I was perfectly unable to move without help and too weak even to hold a glass of water to drink, so had to drink from a reed which was put into my mouth. In the afternoon I was already cold to my shoulders and knees, so Middleton kept applying hot water flannels to the cold parts and over my stomach which did me good and brought me round. I seemed to have lost all memory and even now, the 27th, I am unfit to do the least thing and in addition to the fearful weakness from which I am suffering have dropsy in my feet, legs, stomach and face.

Middleton has been living with Mr. Coillard for several years, but is now returning to England. He left with my wagon and the mission wagon on the 16th January and now to add to all my sickness, I'm very lonely, besides weak, not yet being able to walk 200 yards. Can this loss of blood be caused by over exposure to the sun and rain and the swamps of Luangha and Matondo? the former of which has to be travelled through at night on account of the tsetse fly (it takes three nights to get through). I did it returning in two, staying in the swamp all day and sending the oxen to islands (open) to be out of the way of the fly which infests the bush.

On the 1st February arrived Dr. Dardier[2] of the French mission

[1] The English artisan who came up with Coillard's mission party in 1884.

[2] Dr. Dardier, a Swiss from Geneva, and M. and Mme. Louis Jalla and M. Goy, missionaries, arrived at Sefula to begin work by 20 August 1887. Dardier had sunstroke and fever and in consequence soon returned to Sesheke and Westbeech's station.

party (Coillard's). He has been ill from low fever ever since he arrived in the Barotse Valley last October. He is [of] a very excitable nature and will never pull round here. Well, he asks me to let him stay with me until I go south, and then take him as a passenger. I have agreed, but really do not know how I am going to look after him, being weaker myself and needing as much, if not more care, than he does. However, I have given him a nice cool room and we must do the best we can. No rain ! Don't know how it will go for food with the natives this year. Cannot persuade Dardier to take medicine, neither soup nor meat which I cook for him ; all he will take is milk, wine, jam, preserved grapes in syrup and preserved ginger, all of which are great bilious articles. Now and then he does take a little bread which I give him with milk, or a little wine and water to keep up his strength but medicine he will *not take* except laudanum to give him sleep. The jam and syrup grapes and ginger I have had to forbid. He has also dropsy in his feet, legs and face. I went in for iron tonics and quinine three times daily and am in consequence nearly free from that disorder, but D. will not. As he is a doctor I suppose he knows best, but as experience teaches and I have had both dropsy and fever many times oft, I take what has always done me good and always shall.

Have sent twice to Shesheki to the French Mission, part of which is in that town, for them or one of them to come and see Dardier who is really very bad and seems to be getting worse every day, and in fact I have no hope of his recovery. They say they cannot come,[1] having their own households to look after etc. and as he persisted in coming to Gazungula in spite of their remonstrances, that he must now get on as well as he can. Pleasant for me, who am [my]self in need of nursing. They appear to have washed their hands of all responsibility respecting him, and when I think of the way they left me on our return from the valley, they also returning with two empty wagons and sixteen oxen to each wagon and me with a heavily loaded wagon and only fourteen oxen, I am far from satisfied. Mr. Coillard told his drivers that

[1] Dardier had recently gone to Sesheke to attend Mme. Jalla in childbirth.

January–February, 1888

they must push on and not travel with me, as I would be sticking fast in the mud and then they would have to assist me ;[1] so they left *me* to my own resources to get on as well as I could, and went down to Shesheki where they arrived only three days before me and where I still found them on my arrival there. Well, their oxen are all fly stuck[2] and they have now to rest them and mine are in good condition, and I expect they will have to ask for my driver for help before they arrive at Mangwato (two oxen of their span died before getting to Shesheki and three more before they arrived in Panda Matenga, all fly stuck and the last I heard, that the rest were so weak that they could scarcely with their empty wagon keep up to my loaded one) and I or rather my driver will return good for evil and help them. They would never have been able to leave Gazungula, had I not again have come to the rescue, for they had not, nor could get, a grain of corn or other food from the natives, who are themselves starving, so in spite of all I supplied their wants. And again when I think that through me their mission is established in the country, and I could so easily have settled the Jesuits in the valley, who even offered me £500 to assist them which I refused because I had given my word to Coillard to assist him, it rather riles me. I suppose C. thinks he was doing something grand when he made me the present of the silver watch two years ago. Well, they will want me still for they have no friend in the country but the King and his position is far from secure and he can be murdered or driven out by his people any day—but I think they will have to want this time before I move a finger to assist them again. Such is a sample of missionary gratitude as a rule, and C. has certainly not proved any exception to that rule. However, every dog has his day. Now they have just left Dr. Dardier to get on as well as he can with me, and seem to have no further interest in him, and we are both sick and weak.

On February 23rd Dr. Dardier died in my arms and with the

[1] This was not in the interior tradition of mutual help.
[2] Bitten by the tsetse fly and doomed to die of nagana, the disease of domestic animals transmitted by that insect.

assistance of my boys I buried him, poor fellow. He passed away very peacefully and I think it was for him a happy release. Don't know what they'll now say or think when I send them the news to Shesheki, the very Kafirs talk about their leaving him here, without any of themselves to look after him, but just to my care who am [my]self ill.

26th February. At 8 A.M. Magumpa arrived at my place during very heavy rain. It appears that last night he fled to an island with his wives and servants and all of his town's people who had not fled, news having arrived that the old Maransian whom they had driven out in 85, had stolen a march on Shesheki,[1] killed Tahalima (second headman there), his son, and another Marotse, also fourteen of Magumpa's hunters whom he had caught on the Magelic River, and had seized and driven off all the cattle and men, women and children that he could find on the north side of the Zambesi, and they were afraid he would collect all the Shesheki boats and kill all refugees he could find, so Magumpa being my great friend, and as such I have always found him, thought it best to leave the island and trust to me for assistance in case Maransian crossed the river or should come across him. Food is what I was scarce of for such a lot, so he and his wives and children were provided for by me, and the people who were with him, numbering about sixty of both sexes and of all ages, had to provide for themselves, which they did very thoroughly by robbing the gardens of their townsmen or of any other who had not thrown in their lot with them, but preferring the bush to the open. Nearly all the corn and mealies being fit for gathering, they did very well. I must, however, give them all credit by saying that, although their temporary huts surrounded my mealie gardens, I had not a single mealie robbed, and they were all fit for food. Maransian by report had but fifty men with him, but it was enough to make the whole river, or the inhabitants thereof, from

---

[1] Sikabenga, the Mulasiane ousted in December 1885, took advantage of Lewanika's absence on a raid against the Mashukulumbwe to attack Sesheke. Coillard states that this attack occurred in March 1888, but from this it appears that it happened in February.

February–March, 1888

the Victoria Falls to Katongo (which would number at least five thousand) bolt. Had Magumpa's people been but a shade plucky, Maransian would never have succeeded in recrossing the Magelic on his return to the Batoka country where he is now staying. Magumpa recrosses the river to his own town tomorrow the 4th March and I shall go to visit him in a few days to reassure them, but chiefly to learn any news that may come from Shesheki. Maransian is at least 100 miles from this on his return, but still their funk of him is something both shameful and dreadful. I always knew the Zambesi niggers to be cowards, but never thought them so thoroughly such as I now see them to be.

March 10*th.* Received a letter from the missionaries thanking me for the care I had taken of Dr. D. and sorry for the trouble I had been put up to. Although I wrote them to come or send to get his things, none have yet turned up here to do so.

In the afternoon bought some ivory of Magumpa and on the 11th accompanied him to his town which is only about 10 miles from this. Stayed with him three days, during which time I received two sheep to slaughter and heard that Luwanika was with an army at the Injoko River, en route for the Bashukulumbwe country, but having heard about Maransian's little doings, had started off two regiments on the spoor and that Shesheki people and Magumpa's and all down to the Falls were to join these two regiments, follow up the spoor to where they met the King with the main army at Sagitema's town,[1] when they would then all go on until they got Maransian and the cattle (don't they wish they may get him) and then enter the Bashukulumbwe country from the south east, instead of N.E. Those are the present plans, shall hear sometime how they succeeded. I don't think they will ever get Maransian and I am sure they will not go far to look for him. Forgot to note that on the 2nd March I received a letter from Maransian written for him by one of the missionaries at Shesheki, saying : —

[1] The Batoka chief, on the southeastern borders of the Mashukulumbwe, with whom the Mulasiane was living.

Shooting Norman's Horse – Near Luwale River.
27th Feby. 1876

This incident occurred on the return journey, at a small periodic river, the Lwale, about forty-six miles north of Shoshong. The animal is plainly emaciated, but this may have been caused by horsesickness, a deadly disease of equines peculiar to Africa that was prevalent during the rains. At this time of year the pasture should have been ample. I guess that MacLeod holds the lantern, because he would, no doubt, ask someone else to execute his horse. The water barrel or *vat* is shown on the back of the wagon.

No. 104

Caught in a Trap! Near 'Mpareira. River Chobe.
June 1875

One of the party, probably MacLeod, has fallen into a concealed game pit, an accident that might have had serious consequences if the pit were staked. His white companion is Cowley. The place is near Impalera Island, at the Chobe–Zambezi junction.

No. 100

No. 104

William Frederic Fairlie

Norman Magnus MacLeod

March, 1888

Old Friend, I came to Shesheki to revenge myself on those that wanted to kill me when I was chief of that town, but not succeeding in killing, drove me out, but killing my relatives, my children, and took my wives to themselves. Well, I have succeeded a little for I have killed Tehalima and his son, also Mukeylie's[1] son. I have seized many cattle and made prisoners of many people, but I am not and shall not be satisfied before I have met Luwanika and that before he is killed by his own people, for it is their intention to do so. I am now going but shall return with many Batoka and Matabele, and then let the Barotse have fear of me. With many greetings,

Goodbye, Your child, Maransian.

I myself have an idea that Luwanika's people will on this war either kill him and go over to Maransian or it will not be long before they do one or the other, for if Maransian lives[2] the Barotse will always have to be on the 'qui vive' and prepared for war, and such a state of unquiet will never do for this nation, and again the people are very fond of Maransian and now they are afraid of him, especially as he has with such a small number raided Shesheki, and numbers have already fled to him. Such is at present the state of their happy country.

March 18. Magumpa and all the people he could collect started on the war trail today, only the old men and women, young and old, and those too young to fight or swell the crowd, being left to look after the villages and gardens. When they think of catching up to Maransian, I don't know, for he is already twenty days ahead and supposing he only goes 10 miles a day there's a slight distance between them, and he is more likely to go 20 or more instead of less with his small party, and the Barotse party being afraid of him will go very gingerly. (Maransian calls me father

---

[1] The Mokhole, a Sesheke headman.

[2] The Matabele saved Lewanika the trouble of killing the Mulasiane. Akafuna was murdered by his brother Wamalunga, who was also living at Siachitema's. In August 1888 a Matabele impi crossed the Zambezi with Batoka assistance and attacked the village; they killed the Mulasiane and Wamalunga and many others.

because when I lived at Shesheki in 1874, 75 and 76 his father was my great friend and the present Maransian was then only about ten years old.)

March 22nd. Took a round of three days to get or look for some game. Got as far as the Inguesi River and there shot a sable antelope and arrived home at Gazungula on Sunday noon. One of my buffaloes being fat, had the meat cut up for myself, and the other and sable antelope will do for the boys and dogs, it being chiefly for the latter part I went. Inguesi River one day from this. From Monday to Thursday down with ague. April one of my hunters returned home having seen no elephants, the bush where the elephants stand being full of refugees from Luwanika, who threatens to kill every Matotella and Matoka from Magelic to Mapansa's, a distance of about 200 miles; so what with their dread of him added to their fear of Maransian they have fled all their towns, and their crops which are now ripe are being destroyed by birds and beasts. As it was not safe, April being in the wild with only eight Kafirs, he thought it the best policy to return here until affairs are decided one way or the other, and I think him quite right. Very many Matotella and Matoka have gone on Maransian's trail to join him. News arrived here that Luwanika's intention [was] to kill all the Shesheki people, headmen as well as slaves, also Magumpa; in fact to clear the country from Shesheki to the Victoria Falls, and that it was only by intercession of his Barotse chief men who are related to many down here, that the affair has been stopped. However, it is only stopped for a time, as he has means to accuse them of complicity with Maransian. He has already since I left the valley in December killed four headmen, and unless they kill him or drive him away, he will formally try the Shesheki ones and have them assegaied, as he has long wished to pay off a few old scores that he has amongst them. My opinion is, that the nation will before long declare for Maransian or another named Umurungwi[1] and make him chief and Luwanika will be murdered, not driven away again, for fear of reprisal.

[1] Wamalunga.

March–April, 1888

We shall see! Happy country this. How would you like to be living in it?

April 16*th*. Wagon has been gone now three months to Mangwato for a span of oxen to take me south, but no news of them yet. It is most strange and I am beginning to imagine that some accident may have happened to them along the road.

The Diary of
Captain Norman MacLeod
1875–1876

THE DIARY OF NORMAN MACLEOD

1875–1876

January 19*th*, 1875. Engaged 4 boys, Zulus, for trip to Zambesi at 3/- a month, 2 as foreloupers, 1 cook, 1 groom.

29*th*. Back to Maritzburg.

30*th*. 13th P.A.L.I. marched in, come from Malta, to relieve 75th. Bought pointer 'Clem' for £3-10.

February 1*st*. Bought pointer 'King' £3. Got another, 'Dinah,' from Woodroffe.

5*th*. Bought 12 oxen from Hawkins, £10 each. Zulu, all inoculated.[1]

7*th*. Started at last for our trip to Zambesi. Fairlie, myself, and Cowley,[2] a young fellow out here by way of learning farming. We had a wagon and span of oxen apiece, supplies for a year, 5 or 6 dogs. I had 2 horses, the others 1 each. My wagon stuck on the town hill. The oxen did not know their places, and the boy couldn't drive. Then I broke the disselboom.[3]

9*th*. Got to Howick with difficulty. Halted to get

10*th*. new disselboom. Shot a few ducks & snipe. Rain.

14*th*. Started again at 2.30. Borrowed a driver from a transport rider[4] McIntosh, a good man. Soon put the oxen together. Rain every day. I shall only give a general account, as each day's notes are in the diary (Letts)[5] for 1875.

16*th*. Got into a tremendous hail storm as we were going to outspan. Stones as big as bullets fell. Hurt my head and frightened

---

[1] Zulu oxen, a small native breed of cattle that was very hardy. They were inoculated against lungsickness, or pleuropneumonia, a disease of cattle introduced into South Africa in 1854. The yellow virus from the lungs of an animal dead of the disease was allowed to soak into a piece of twine, which was passed through a hole punched in the skin of the tail just above the tuft, tied in a loop, and left there. This induced a mild form of the malady, though it sometimes resulted in a loss of the tail.

[2] Dr. Holub calls him Frank Cowley, but his name appears to have been Richard.

[3] The wagon pole.   [4] One who freighted for hire, by ox wagon.

[5] This diary has not been found.

the horses. I was riding one and leading the other, but it broke away and I was half the night catching it. Passed Estcourt on 17th. A pretty little place on Bushmans River. Got a few duck & snipe.

19*th*. Reached Colenso on Tugela R. Lost one hound 'Don.' Dined at hotel kept by Capt. Dickinson late 83rd Regt. Tugela full. Crossed in punt. About 100 yds. across. Thermometer 84. Halted wagons where road to Ladysmith turns off. Rode there to try and get a driver. There is a colony of Hottentots, Christians, who are all drivers. Saw plenty. Offered £4 a month but none would come.

26*th*. To top of Drachensberg (by Van Reenans Pass), a long range quite inaccessible except at one or two places and very steep there. Weather very bad, constant rain, and hot. Thermometer 94 and in sun 110 but much cooler on top. Reached Wilja R. on 27th, too full to cross. Had to wait to cross. Shot a few duck & snipe.

March 1*st*. Harrismith, a good sized place with plenty of stores. Cold in winter, being so near the berg.[1] Snow lies on the ground. Horses can be bought cheap. Engaged a Totty,[2] Andries, as driver for £3 a month.

4*th*. Trekked on again and saw game for the first time in the shape of a few spring bok. F. bought a pony and we lost our best pointer, 'King.' Crossed Wilga R. again at Bowsers drift. Had to offload, and send things over in punt, wagons by ford.

7*th*. Fine weather set in now. Fired several shots at spring bok & blesbok, without success, also saw ostriches. Fine undulating grass country. No wood. We now travelled steadily on to Potchefstroom, crossing the Vaal River by punt, trekking twice a day at daylight and in afternoon, using cow dung for our fires. We saw springbok & blesbok every day, but only once in great numbers. There it was what Gordon Cumming[3] has described, thousands &

---

[1] The Drakensberg.   [2] A Hottentot.

[3] R. Gordon Cumming, author of *Five Years of a Hunter's Life in the Far Interior of South Africa* (London, 1850), a famous Nimrod who hunted in Bechuanaland, the Orange Free State, and the Transvaal during the 1840's.

March–April, 1875

thousands and wildebeest also, a wonderful sight. It was bad luck
for me as in galloping after them my horse put his foot in a hole
and rolled over. I got a really bad fall, broke my collar bone, and
damaged my right side and arm, so that I couldn't move it for 3
weeks. We only got 1 blesbok & 1 springbok, but plenty of
coran.[1] Potchefstroom is a large place on a plain surrounded by
hills. Road hedged with willows & figs. No life about it, but a
good many stores, mostly new and kept by English. The gold
fields[2] have increased the business here. 34 days from Howick,
about 320 miles.

27th. Zeerust, having trekked over same sort of ground since
Potchefstroom, open, lots of coran & occasional springbok, etc.
Have had a good deal of rain. Zeerust is a trading station, a rising
place, 2 churches, 2 or 3 stores, etc. at the head of the L. Marico.[3]
Supplies traders & Boer farmers. Cold here sometimes. Frost &
snow. Trekked on over high hills into Marico valley. Found
several farms, one just taken by an Englishman, a draper. He gave
£400 for the farm, 4000 morgen, and is doing well. This Marico
used to be Moselikatse's,[4] the Matabele country, but the Boers
drove them further on. Lots of small game along Marico R. Saw
also a few sassaby & pallah & 3 ostriches. River pretty, above 70
yds. across, full of crocodiles, thick bush. Passed junction of
Marico & Crocodile.[5] Saw quagga, waterbuck, springbok &
wildebeest. Country sandy with acres of low thorns. Crossed Not-
wani R., an apology for a river, nearly dry now with fine trees on
banks. Saw koodoo & quagga. I got a shot at a lion the first day I
carried a gun, 26 days after my fall, but missed. If I had had the
proper use of my arm, I don't think I could have missed.

April 14th. Arrived at Bamangwato exactly 2 months from Ho-

[1] *Korhaan*, or bustard.
[2] The newly discovered gold deposits in the eastern Transvaal.
[3] The Klein Marico River.
[4] Mzilikazi, first king and founder of the Matabele nation, broke away from the
Zulus circa 1821 and went to live in what is now the western Transvaal. He was
driven from that country by the Boers of the Great Trek in 1837–1838; he travelled
north with his people and made a new home in Matabeleland, Southern Rhodesia.
[5] The Limpopo River.

wick, about 660 miles. I lost my best horse 'Guts' from inflamma-
tion of lungs[1] yesterday. Saw our first giraffe yesterday also.
Bamangwato is a trading station with several stores. Most of the
Zambesi traders load up & start from here. It is also a Kafir town,
the capital of the Bechuana nation. Population said to be 10,000.
Kama the present King is about 45 & seems a nice, intelligent
fellow. He is a Christian and dresses as if to walk in Rotten Row.
He is now stopping Boers coming in to hunt as they kill off everything for skins and he will not allow liquor to be taken in. The
trade is feathers & ivory.

16*th*. Left Bamangwato for the *Zambesi* in company with George
Dorehill, a young fellow who had been trading and hunting for 3
or 4 years. I will not continue daily records, which are in Letts
diary for 1875 but just state generally that we travelled by the
western and more direct road by the Kari Kari,[2] leaving the road
for a bit and following the R. Nata from the drift to Matlomo-
ganyani[3] into road again. A great deal was heavy sand, and slow
travelling, also long distances without water (once 3 days) and
water generally only muddy pools. The weather was beautiful,
not too hot.

Fairlie & Cowley each lost a horse close to Bamangwato, after
which we had no sickness either amongst horses or oxen. We
hunted every day and had fair sport, chiefly giraffe, but also buffalo, eland, quagga, koodoo, sable antelope, wildebeest, springbok,
& elephant on the Nata R. and a rhinoceros. Also lots of pheasants, partridges, & guinea fowl. The thermometer in April &
May were to vary from about 80 to 100 in the wagon during the
day, from about 50 to 70 at daylight, but in June it got down to 44
at daybreak.

On the 13th June we arrived at Pantamatinka where the Zambesi traders leave their wagons while trading across the river.

[1] The African horsesickness. See sketch 100.
[2] This road led north from Shoshong past the eastern side of the Makarikari Salt
Pan, and joined the Westbeech Road from Tati at Nwasha Pan.
[3] Matlamanyane, a chain of four permanent waters on the road to the Zambezi.
Nwasha Pan was the last of these towards the north.

Pantamatinka is about 400 miles from Bamangwato, and about 60 from the Zambesi at Impareira,[1] where the Chobe joins, and where the crossing is. Wagons come within 12 miles of the river crossing through 2 narrow belts of fly (tsetse)[2] in the night, but go back to remain at Pantamatinka where we left ours for 7 months.

We waited on the Zambesi 5 weeks for permission from Sepopa, King of the Barotse people, to visit him, at Sesheke his capital on the northern bank and 60 miles up river. After the dearth of water it was a great pleasure to be camped on the river, to bathe every day, and have good water to drink. We shot a few buffalo, and there were elephants about, but we could not follow them, as we expected messengers from the King every day. One night a large troop of elephants came within 30 yds. of our camp, but it was too dark. We could not see even the outline.

At last we got to Sesheke in canoes. Our idea was to get shooting on the north side, where game is abundant, as no one can cross the river ever without the King's permission, and no white men hunt there, but the King's idea was to get all out of us he could, and give us nothing in return. After some time he sent us up the river to shoot sea cow. We saw several, but could not get one. Then another delay, and he sent us about 40 miles inland north for elephants, but he took care not to send us to a good place. We saw one troop. I shot one, an enormous one, tusks about 100 lbs. each, 7 ft. 5 in. long, but the King did not give them to me. We saw great quantities of other game of all sorts. Cowley shot two lions,[3] but the game on the Zambesi flats on this bank of river was a marvellous sight, leche & pookoo buck, wildebeest & quagga, also buffalo.

Hearing wonderful stories of the annual elephant hunt which

[1] Impalera Island and Village. See note 2, page 32.
[2] The tsetse fly, which was confined to relatively well-defined areas. It transmits nagana, a virulent disease of domestic animals, hence the need to protect the oxen by crossing fly belts in darkness, when the fly is inactive.
[3] Cowley was anxious to make a name as a lion hunter. In September, when he asked Sipopa where he could shoot lions, the King told him he seemed too young for it, but that his people would show him the animals. Four Africans took Cowley to the left bank of the Kasaya River, where he killed a lion that charged him determinedly.

takes place at the beginning of the rains, when the river is lowest, when they kill, we were told, 300 elephants in one day on the flat in the angle of Zambesi & Chobe, we determined to see it, so arranged to go back to wagons to see all right, come back to Sesheke, and from there go down river to Victoria Falls before the hunt. So on 16th August started back to wagons and on 5th September got back to Sesheke again.[1] I lost a great deal of game on Zambesi by smashing my favourite rifle and having to shoot with another, which I found after several unaccountable misses was sighted all on one side.

As soon as I got to Sesheke, I had a slight attack of fever and ague, followed by a severe attack of dropsy in the legs, which kept me literally on my back for 21 days, and stopped our going to the Falls. I was there some time before I could walk, but was just able to join in the elephant hunt,[2] which was arranged for the 29th October, and which duly came off but was a failure. However it was worth seeing. There were over 200 canoes on river at once, and about 2000 men. The system of hunting is by fire, beaters etc. to drive the elephants up to the King and party, about 200, who receive them with a volley and then everyone attacks with guns & assegais. But they let the mass of the elephants break back. We only saw 14 and killed 9, but the 14 were all bulls with good ivory, and it was fine to see them come on. They were turned on all sides, and finally charged in a clump down on our party of 200 men. When within 100 yds. they received a volley, but if Sepopa had let them come to 30 yds. they ought all to have been dropped.

Next day I saw about 100 elephants. Instead of shooting came back and told the King, but his hunters made a mess of it, and we never saw them again. Next day went a long way into angle where Chobe & Zambesi join, but elephants had crossed river. Were

---

[1] MacLeod, Fairlie, and Cowley were at Lesuma on 1 September 1875. Dr. Holub, who was en route to Pandamatenga, met them there, and they sent two of MacLeod's horses back with him, in charge of a servant. A lion killed one of the horses at night.

[2] MacLeod, Fairlie, Cowley, and Dorehill attended this hunt. Sipopa was at first reluctant to permit them to go, but at last he furnished a canoe to take them.

caught in heavy thunderstorm, hail & rain, bitterly cold. Several niggers died that night. We then returned to Sesheke, and as soon after as possible got boats to M'Pareira, and back to wagons. The King did not treat us well going away, having got all he could out of us. He would not give me the big tusks I shot, which he had promised to give, and I had given him a valuable horse, beads, 2 rifles. etc.

24th November. Got back to wagons.[1] Soon after started with Fairlie for Victoria Falls, got fever on road, nearly died in the bush. Charlie, our best boy, did die. Then F. got it and finally we got back to wagons having been for weeks within 8 miles of the Falls, without ever seeing them. We found every one at Pantamatinka had also had fever and poor Cowley was dead. He died on 19th Dec. After a weary time of semi-starvation and slow attempts at recovery, I started again for the Falls with Dorehill, leaving Fairlie who was not well enough. We hired donkeys from Wisbeach and rode. We got there but were attacked with fever & ague, and had a fearful time of it, only just succeeding in getting back to wagons alive. After some further time, as soon as we could muster a strong enough party to inspan, we started south again on 20th February 1876.

Travelled same road back to Bamangwato. Found water very scarce, and very hard up for food. Had to keep the boys on very short rations. Had fever & ague on and off the whole way down, and were all weak & ill. I got tossed on horseback by an old buffalo bull. I got off, but horse was killed, and not the buffalo.[2]

Trekked into Bamangwato on 1st March, where we stayed till 7th getting my wagon [tires] shortened, the tires being about an

---

[1] Westbeech, Dorehill, and Cowley left Sesheke for Pandamatenga on 10 November, but Sipopa refused to let MacLeod and Fairlie go. However, he gave them canoes soon afterwards.

[2] On the Nata River. His horse was hit from behind by the buffalo, and horse and rider were thrown down. MacLeod was lying helpless in a thorn bush while the buffalo gored his horse to death. It then decamped without harming the man. (Millais, *Life of F. C. Selous*, London, 1919, p. 110.)

inch off the wood all round.[1] Trekked steadily on by Crocodile R. & Marico to Zeerust on 22nd. Crossed Vaal R. on 5th April at Christiana and outspanned outside Kimberley Diamond Fields on 11th. Large, busy place, all canvas and corrugated iron. Colesberg Kopje one big hole 1000 yds. round, 2 to 300 ft. deep. Remained 4 days here, then by Boshoff, Winburg to Harrismith on 6th May. Stopped one day and on arriving at Maritzburg on the 16th May having been away exactly 15 months and 10 days. Only stayed long enough to sell wagons etc. Got 8/6 a lb. for ivory.

30 *June*. Embarked on Florence. Shifted on 6th at Algoa Bay to Edinburgh Castle, Capt. Penford. Touched at Madeira and arrived at Plymouth on 30 July 1876.

[1] The wagon wheels were bound with flat iron tires. The wood of the wheels had shrunk in the dry air, leaving the tires loose.

BIBLIOGRAPHY

1. 'An Old Harrovian' [Percy C. Reid], 'After Big Game in Southern-Central Africa.' *The Field* (London), Vol. 67, March 27, 1886, pp. 392–93.

2. Arnot (F. S.) *Garenganze: or, Seven Years' Pioneer Mission Work in Central Africa.* New York & Chicago: Fleming H. Revell, n.d. [1889].

3. Berghegge (Father Francis, S. J.) 'Account of a Journey in Central Africa.' *Rhodesiana No. 3* (Salisbury), 1958, pp. 1–13.

4. Bertrand (Alfred) *The Kingdom of the Barotsi, Upper Zambezia.* London: T. Fisher Unwin, 1899.

5. Bradshaw (Dr. Benjamin F.) 'Notes on the Chobe River, South Central Africa.' *Proceedings of the Royal Geographical Society* (London), New Series, Vol. III, 1881, pp. 208–13 and map.

6. *Burke's Landed Gentry.* London, 1939.

7. Coillard (François) *On the Threshold of Central Africa. A Record of Twenty Years' Pioneering among the Barotsi of the Upper Zambesi.* London: Hodder and Stoughton, 1897.

8. Cooper-Chadwick (J.) *Three Years with Lobengula.* London: Cassell and Co., n.d.

9. Dawnay (Hon. Guy) Unpublished diary, Matabeleland and the Zambezi, 1873.

10. Decle (Lionel) *Three Years in Savage Africa.* London: Methuen and Co., 1898.

11. Fairlie (W. F.) Unpublished diaries, Morocco, May–June 1871 and South Africa, April–September 1873.

12. ——'Hippopotamus Shooting near Quilimane.' *The Field* (London), Vol. 56, September 18, 1880, pp. 437–38.

13. ——'Elephant Shooting in S.E. Africa.' *The Field* (London), August 1881.

14. ——'Shooting in South Africa.' *The Field* (London), July 1882.

15. ——'Elephant Shooting on Lake Nyassa.' *The Field* (London), Vol. 61, January 6, 1883, pp. 23–24.

16. Gibbons (Capt. A. St. H.) 'A Journey in the Marotse and Mashikolumbwe Countries.' *The Geographical Journal* (London), Vol. 9, February 1897, pp. 121–143.

17. ——*Exploration and Hunting in Central Africa, 1895–96*. London : Methuen and Co., 1898.

18. Hole (H. Marshall) *The Passing of the Black Kings*. London : Philip Allan, 1932.

19. Holub (Dr. Emil) 'Lion Adventures in Central South Africa.' *The Field* (London), Vol. 55, January 10, 1880, p. 40.

20. ——*Seven Years in South Africa*. London : Sampson Low, Marston, Searle, and Rivington, 1881. 2 volumes.

21. Lacy (George) 'Pioneer Hunters, Traders, and Explorers of South Africa.' *South Africa* (London), 29 weekly numbers, 12 January to 21 September, 1895.

22. MacLeod (Norman) Unpublished diary, 1863–1880.

23. ——A note on his trip to the Zambezi. *The Field* (London), Vol. 47, June 3, 1876, p. 630.

24. Millais (J. G.) *Life of Frederick Courtenay Selous*. London & New York : Longmans, Green and Co., 1919.

25. Oates (Frank) *Matabele Land and the Victoria Falls*. London : C. Kegan Paul and Co., 1881.

26. Pinto (Major Serpa) *How I Crossed Africa*. Philadelphia : J. B. Lippincott and Co., 1881. 2 volumes.

27. 'Regulus' [H. A. Cripwell] 'Rhodesia. Some Account of Places and Events.' *The Shield* (Salisbury), No. 133, February 1957, pp. 8–11.

28. Reid (Percy C.) 'Journeys in the Linyanti Region.' *The Geographical Journal* (London), Vol. 17, June 1901, pp 573–88.

29. Schulz (A.) and A. Hammar *The New Africa*. London : William Heinemann, 1897.

BIBLIOGRAPHY

30. Selous (F. C.) *A Hunter's Wanderings in Africa*. London : Richard Bentley and Son, 1881.

31. ——'Letters from Mr. F. C. Selous on His Journeys to the Kafukwe River, and on the Upper Zambesi.' *Proceedings of the Royal Geographical Society* (London), New Series, Vol. XI, 1889, pp. 216–23 and map.

32. ——*Travel and Adventure in South-East Africa*. London : Rowland Ward and Co., 1893.

33. Starkey (John R.) 'A Shooting Trip North of the Zambesi.' *The Field* (London), Vol. 71, February 4, 1888, p. 142.

34. Tabler (Edward C., editor) *Zambezia and Matabeleland in the Seventies*. London : Chatto and Windus, 1960.

35. Tylden (Major G.) *The Armed Forces of South Africa*. Johannesburg : The Africana Museum, 1954.

36. Wallis (J. P. R., editor) *The Northern Goldfields Diaries of Thomas Baines*. London : Chatto and Windus, 1946. 3 volumes.

37. ——*The Barotseland Journal of James Stevenson-Hamilton*, 1898–1899. London : Chatto and Windus, 1953.

38. ——*The Southern African Diaries of Thomas Leask*, 1865–1870. London : Chatto and Windus, 1954.

39. *Who Was Who*. London & New York, 1941.

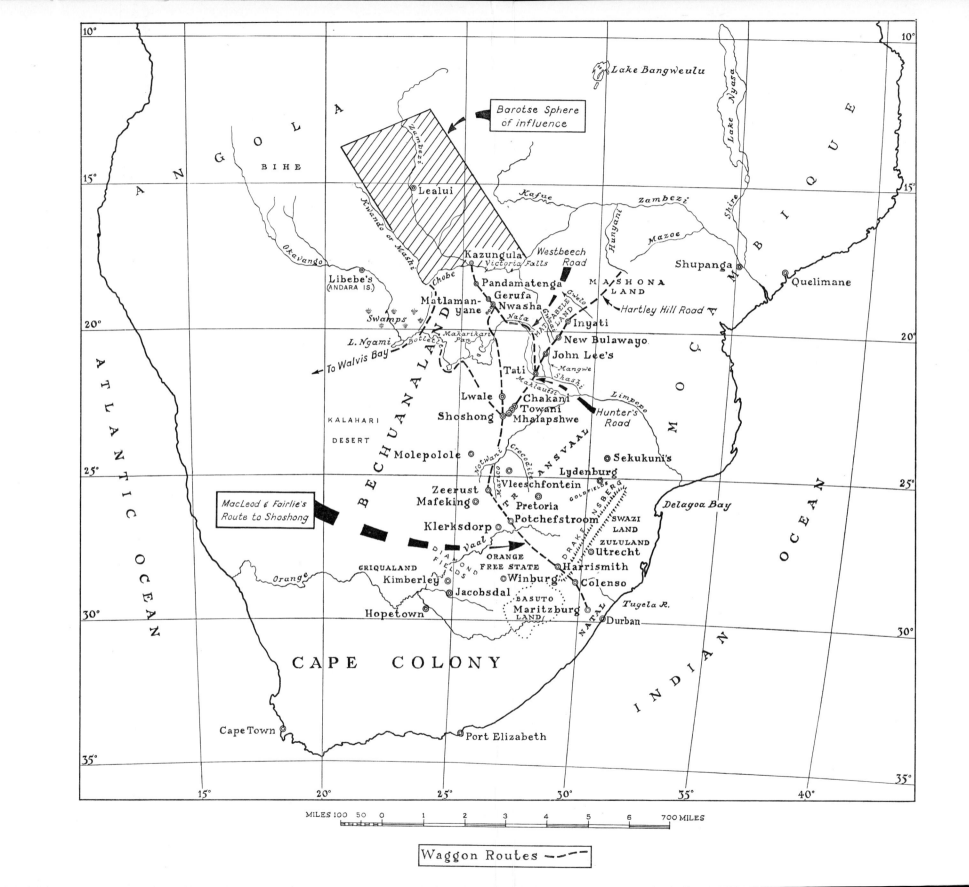

INDEX

A

Aden, 14

Adonis, 59, 61, 63, 65

Administrator of North-Western Rhodesia, 10

Africa (coloured hunter), 59, 63, 71

Akufuna, *see* Tatila

Albania, 12

Algoa Bay, 112

Allen, Brother, 30

A-Luyi, 1

Andara Island, 45

Andaman Islands, 12

Angola, 1, 4, 31, 52

Angolans, 7

Andries (hunter to Westbeech), 59, 71

Andries (servant to MacLeod), 106

April (hunter), 59, 71, 100

Arnot, F. S., 6

August (hunter), 59–60, 63, 72

Austrian, 55, 76

Ayrshire Yeomanry, 16

B

Baila, 2, 29, 49, 53

Baines, Thomas, 77

Bamangwato, 20–1, 25, 31, 107–9, 111

Band, 36–7

Bangweolo, Lake, 32

Bano Gha, *see* Banosha

Banosha, 44–5

Barkly, Sir Henry, 29

Barlow, Sir Morrison, 16

Barotse, 1–4, 6–8, 10–11, 28, 30–1, 35, 38–9, 42, 44, 49–50, 53–4, 56, 61, 63, 68, 70, 73–4, 80, 83–84, 88, 90, 94, 99–100

Barotse, council of state, 7

Barotseland, 2, 5–7, 17–18, 27–8, 32, 36, 38, 45

Bashukulumbwe, *see* Mashukulumbwe

Batoka, 3–4, 29–30, 33, 76, 97, 99–100

Bechuana, 20, 43, 45, 108

Bechuanaland, 2, 33, 36, 52–3, 106

Benguella, 49

Bihé, 4

Blesbok, 106–7

Blockley, George, 5–7, 39, 51

Bob (African carrier), 62

Boers, 15, 107–8

Booms, Father, 30

Boshoff, 112

Bowsers Drift, 106

Bradshaw, Doctor Benjamin Frederick, 6

British, 3–5, 8–9, 12

British South Africa Company, 10

Brock, 29

Buffalo, 42–3, 50, 56, 59–68, 71–2, 76, 80, 83, 88, 100, 108–9, 111

Bulawayo, 26, 30, 77

Bumbui, 11

Burgers, Fort, 15

Burma, 12

Bushmen, 26, 57, 60, 63, 65, 67, 71–2

Bushmens River, 106

C

D

E

F

INDEX

Joros, *see* Westbeech
Jurua, *see* Gerufa

K

Kabompo River, 1, 91
Kabompo District, 4
Kabuku, 56
Kachila, 89
Kafue, 3, 34, 49, 53, 76
Kali, 11, 88
Kalkfontein, 9
Kama, *see* Khama
Kari Kari, *see* Makarikari
Kasaya Channel, 59
Kasaya River, 109
Katima Mulilo, 11, 58, 64, 82–3
Katonga, 2, 11, 42, 50, 56, 80–1, 89, 97
Katongo, *see* Katonga
Katukula, 40
Kazungula, 11, 38, 45, 54, 59, 81–82, 89, 92–5, 100
Kenya, 10
Khama, 20, 49, 108
Khame, *see* Khama
Khami River, 27
Khazuma Flat, 87
Kilwa, 13
Kimberley, 36, 98, 112
King of Barotseland, 1, 7–8, 10, 33, 35–6, 39–40, 42, 44, 46–7, 49, 50–1, 54, 56, 62, 67, 69–70, 73, 75, 78, 80–2, 84–5, 88–92, 95, 97, 109–11
King of the Matabele, 26
Klaas, old, 59, 62, 65–6
Klaas, young, 59, 62, 65–6
Klein Marico River, 107, 112
Klerksdorp, 29, 31, 77, 90
Koodoo, *see* Kudu
Kroot, Father, 30

Kudu, 44, 107–8
Kwando, 2, 7, 32, 34, 45, 52
Kwena, 2

L

Ladysmith, 106
Lancers, 17th, 12
Langalibalele, 13
Leask, 77
Lealui, 1, 10–11, 33, 35, 44, 46–7, 49–51, 91
Lebebi, *see* Libebe
Leboche, *see* Lewanika
Lechi, *see* Lechwe
Lechulatebe, 43, 91
Lechwe, 56, 89, 91–2, 109
Lee, John, 89
Leopard, 92
Le Koguani, 50
Leshoma, *see* Lesuma
Leshuma, *see* Lesuma
Lesuma, 28, 29, 33–4, 38–9, 49, 51, 54–5
Leteah, *see* Litia
Lewanika, 7–9, 28–30, 32–5, 40, 44, 46, 49–50, 54, 63, 67, 70, 73, 81–2, 88, 91, 96–7, 99–100
Li-a-Liue, *see* Lealui
Libebe, 45–6
Limpopo River, 3, 25, 107, 112
Linyanti, 3–4, 32, 34, 45, 49, 51–2, 54–6, 63–4, 66–7, 70, 72–3, 81–2, 84–5, 89
Lion, 30, 49, 61, 66, 71–2, 80, 92, 107, 109
Litia, 45, 50–1, 54–5
Livingstone, David, 3–4, 31, 47, 63
Lobengula, 5, 7, 9, 26, 76–7, 81
London, 5, 10
London Missionary Society, 2, 4

INDEX